Freedom Riders

John Lewis and Jim Zwerg on the Front Lines of the Civil Rights Movement

COLORED
WAITING ROOM
PRIVATE PROPERTY
NO PARKING
Driving through or Turning Around
CAROLINA

Freedom Riders

John Lewis and Jim Zwerg on the Front Lines of the Civil Rights Movement

by Ann Bausum

NATIONAL GEOGRAPHIC

WASHINGTON, D.C.

For my parents
Dolores and Henry
who raised me up right in the South
and taught me to ask questions

Published by the National Geographic Society

John M. Fahey, Jr., President and Chief Executive Officer

Gilbert M. Grosvenor, Chairman of the Board

Nina D. Hoffman, Executive Vice President, President of Books and Education Publishing Group

Ericka Markman, Senior Vice President, President of Children's Books and Education Publishing Group

Stephen Mico, Publisher, Vice President of Children's Books and Education Publishing Group

Staff for This Book

Nancy Laties Feresten, Vice President, Editor-in-Chief of Children's Books

Bea Jackson, Design Director, Children's Books and Education Publishing Group

Margaret Sidlosky, Illustrations Director, Children's Books and Education Publishing Group

Jennifer Emmett, Project Editor

Marty Ittner, Designer

Priyanka Lamichhane, Editorial Assistant

Jean Cantu, Illustrations Coordinator

Carl Mehler, Director of Maps

Gregory Ugiansky and XNR Productions, Map Research and Production

Rebecca E. Hinds, Managing Editor

R. Gary Colbert, Production Director

Lewis R. Bassford, Production Manager

Vincent P. Ryan, Manufacturing Manager

Printed in the United States of America

Book design by Marty Ittner
The body text of the book is set in Sabon and Helvetica Neue Condensed.

The display text is set in Dirty House.

Library of Congress Cataloging-in-Publication Data

Bausum, Ann.
    Freedom Riders: John Lewis and Jim Zwerg on the front lines of the civil rights movement / by Ann Bausum; forewords by Freedom Riders Congressman John Lewis and Jim Zwerg.
        p. cm.
    Includes bibliographical references and index.
    Trade ISBN 0-7922-4173-8
    Library Binding ISBN 0-7922-4174-6
    1. African American civil rights workers—Biography—Juvenile literature. 2. Civil rights workers—United States—Biography—Juvenile literature. 3. Lewis, John, 1940 Feb. 21—Juvenile literature. 4. Zwerg, Jim, 1939—Juvenile literature. 5. African Americans—Civil rights—Southern States—History—20th century—Juvenile literature. 6. Civil rights movements—Southern States—History—20th century—Juvenile literature. 7. Southern States—Race relations—Juvenile literature. I. Title.
    E185.96.B355 2006
        323'.092'273—dc22   2005012947

Front cover: The first waves of Freedom Riders encountered violence, destruction (bottom photo), and arrests during 1961. Even so, other riders came forward to continue the protest against segregation. Some gathered in distant places such as New York City (top photo) then headed south.

Half title page: Instead of defeating the Freedom Rides, the burning of this Greyhound bus on May 14, 1961, outside Anniston, Alabama, inspired students from Nashville, Tennessee—including John Lewis and Jim Zwerg—to continue them.

Full title page: Before the Freedom Rides, whites and African Americans (often called "colored" then) traveled in segregated parts of public vehicles (with blacks being sent to the back) and used separate waiting rooms, restaurants, and rest rooms in terminals. The photo shown dates from 1940, the year John Lewis was born.

Contents

FOREWORDS

"If not us, then who? If not now, then when? Will there be a better day for it tomorrow or next year? Will it be less dangerous then? Will someone else's children have to risk their lives instead of us risking ours?"

—John Lewis
*May 16, 1961, to other Nashville students
considering joining the Freedom Rides*

By Jim Zwerg

Why did I participate in the Freedom Rides? The answer is simple. It was the right thing to do. When I and other students in Nashville learned about the attacks on the first Freedom Riders, we knew we could not permit violence to defeat social progress. We had to continue the ride. We spent long hours working out the logistics, then the time came to decide who would make up the team. Eighteen students volunteered. I was one of the ten who were chosen.

Was I scared? Yes. But there are some things worth putting your life on the line for. I knew our cause was right and just. I believed deeply that we were on the side of goodness and truth. I was never so certain that I was living my faith as God intended. John Lewis and I came to this same realization from different backgrounds and via different paths. But once we committed ourselves to non-violent direct action, we were no longer two individual activists. We were part of a nationwide force for change, driven by the power of love, faith, and destiny.

It may seem like our lives revolve around great moments, but great moments frequently catch us unaware. Often they first appear to be small and insignificant. Only over time does their impact and significance grow. Great moments in any life may grow from the smallest of good intentions. I find it's the day-to-day acts of kindness, caring, giving, and loving that really make a difference in peoples' lives. You don't have to participate in a sit-in or go on a Freedom Ride to make a difference. You can help make our society and our world better. Look around you. See what needs to be done in your school, neighborhood, city, or state. Make a decision to do something about it. Then take action. The seemingly small "first step" you take today may have a profound and lasting impact for good in someone's life.

The Freedom Rides and the Nashville Student Movement transformed my life. I received so much more than I ever gave. My life was, and is, blessed!

By John Lewis

Captured in the pages of this book is a compelling moment in human history, the drama of the Freedom Rides, the most untold story of the civil rights movement. This is a true account about a band of courageous Americans who were prepared to die for what they believed. Many of us were very young, but we were imbued with the discipline and philosophy of non-violence expounded by Dr. Martin Luther King, Jr., and practiced by Mohandas Gandhi.

We called this crusade the Freedom Rides, but it was more than just a ride for freedom. It was a ride meant to awaken the heart of America to the injustice of its own laws and traditions. It was a ride meant to stir the souls in the Deep South to listen to the cries of their own conscience. It was a ride meant to inspire the local and indigenous people to gather their courage to stand up and speak out for equality in America. It was a ride meant to erode the barriers we all build between each other. It was a ride meant to help create a truly interracial democracy, what we called the Beloved Community, a nation at peace with itself.

There was a spirit within us that would not die. The forces of hatred and violence tried to burn it out of us in Anniston. They tried to beat it out of us in Montgomery. They tried to jail it out of us through the cold and lonely humiliations of Parchman penitentiary in Mississippi, but nothing could destroy our commitment to see the Freedom Rides through.

In a matter of a few incredible months, the Freedom Rides brought an end to decades of segregation in public transportation all across the American South. Those signs that said *White Waiting / Colored Waiting*, *White Men / Colored Men*, and *White Women / Colored Women* that stained the walls of bus stations and train stations across this nation came down. The only place you will see them today is in a museum. Our commitment, our courage, our determination to make our ideals a reality changed this nation forever.

The success of the Freedom Rides inspired hundreds and thousands of children, teenagers, and college students to become a part of the civil rights movement. They participated in campaigns in Mississippi, in Alabama, in Georgia, in Maryland and other parts of the South to win the right to vote. It has always been fascinating to me that one simple means of transportation played such a major role in transforming America. But the most important lesson of the Freedom Rides is that you can do it, too.

Our country needs you. It needs your drive, your dedication, your creativity, your ideas. Whatever it is you care about—whether it is saving the environment, world peace, equal justice under the law, or accessible health care—find your passion and make a difference. You, too, can bring about a revolution of values, a revolution of ideas that can help this nation meet its highest destiny. You can change the world.

INTRODUCTION

This book is all about journeys. Some of them are marked by miles, others by time. Some are marked by what has changed, others by what has not. They all begin in a world of black and white, or, more precisely, in two worlds—one black and one white.

On the night of May 16, 1961, a handful of college students in Tennessee prepared for a difficult journey through those black and white worlds. Many wrote parting letters or made final phone calls to family members they feared they might never see again. Then, with more courage than most people will ever be forced to muster, they boarded a Greyhound bus and headed into the Deep South. One fact made their journey particularly dangerous. These young men and women—blacks and whites alike—intended to sit together and eat together wherever they pleased. Their plans were perfectly legal according to national law but completely at odds with the Southern custom of the segregation, or separation, of the races. The young people—who called themselves Freedom Riders—planned to change all of that. If not, they planned to die trying.

Each Freedom Rider played a notable role in that journey, but this book focuses on two participants in particular, two men who followed very different journeys before meeting up in the pages of history. John Lewis grew up black in the segregated South. Jim Zwerg grew up white in a part of the country that knew little about diversity. The opening chapters of this book let readers compare and contrast these two worlds. Later chapters detail the shared Freedom Ride of John Lewis and Jim Zwerg. This ride covered more than miles. It helped bridge the divide between the black and white worlds. Readers will discover that it even altered the life journeys of participants, one of whom went on to become a member of the U.S. Congress. I am indebted to Jim Zwerg and John Lewis for trusting me with their stories.

I have taken a journey with this book, too. My journey started in the same place and at almost the same time as the Freedom Rides, for I was

Sometimes Freedom Riders journeyed without any help from law enforcement officials. At other times, heavily armed troops served as escorts (above). In either case participants remained alert for trouble.

born in Tennessee just four years before the rides. I've grown up through a world of segregated schools that became integrated and a skin-conscious world that became character conscious. In order to write this book, I drove through my own memories even as I retraced the paths of the Freedom Riders and visited the places touched by their travels.

A note about terminology is in order as readers prepare to journey with this book through the history of the Freedom Rides. Many words have been used to describe people of color. I use "black" and "African American" interchangeably and with equal respect in the pages that follow. Older terms, some equally respectful at one time and some that never were well intentioned, will appear when they contribute to an understanding of the past. Even language takes a journey in these pages.

John Robert Lewis was born at his parents' home on February 21, 1940, near Troy, Alabama. His grandmother served as midwife for the birth. Troy was the county seat of Pike County, an agricultural center in the rich "black belt" of Alabama farmland. Pike County's population peaked at about 32,500 people the year Lewis was born. African Americans (known then as Negroes) made up nearly half of that total.

"Get on board, children, children.
Get on board, children, children.
Get on board, children, children.
Let's fight for human rights."

— *freedom song*

Black America

YOUNG JOHN ROBERT LEWIS wanted to get out of Alabama in the worst way. He wanted to leave behind the state that placed limits on his life just because of the color of his skin. Lewis and his cousin, Della Mae, planned the perfect escape. The children agreed to saw down one of the towering pine trees by their homes and fashion it into a bus. "We were gonna make a bus, and we were gonna roll out of Alabama," recalls the grown Lewis, smiling. Lewis and his cousin knew that "somehow we needed to get out. If we could just make this bus...we'd be all right."

Lewis and Della Mae never made their wooden vehicle, but, years later, Lewis did ride a bus out of Alabama. This one featured rubber-rimmed wheels, not wooden ones. It carried him to Tennessee where he became the first member of his family to attend college. "It seems

Neither of the homes from John Lewis's childhood remain standing today, and no photographs survive of them. The collections of the nearby Troy Public Library include an image (above) of a simple rural home from that era. Lewis's home was equally plain.

Another photo from the Troy Public Library (right) shows Pike County cotton pickers. "Eight to ten hours of stooping like that and your back would be on fire," recalls Lewis, who picked cotton with his family.

"*The world I knew as a little boy was a rich, happy one....We were poor—dirt poor—but I didn't realize it. It was a small world, a safe world, filled with family and friends.*"

—*John Lewis, 1998*

like buses have had a great deal to do with my life," notes Lewis.

John Lewis took his first bus ride while attending Dunn's Chapel Elementary School. He became a student at this two-room school in 1945 at the age of five. The simple building was within walking distance of his home. It had no playground equipment, no furnace, no running water, and no bathrooms. Water was hauled by the bucketful from a neighbor's well three blocks away. Students used an outhouse in place of indoor toilets. Gathering firewood for the wood-burning stove was a class assignment. The students had two teachers—one for each of the building's two classrooms, three grades to a room.

Teachers and students at Dunn's Chapel Elementary shared one fact in common: all of them were, in the language of the times, colored, or Negroes. Like other African-American students in segregated schools, these children used hand-me-down textbooks from the local white schools. When young John Lewis and his classmates took a field trip to the Tuskegee Institute, they rode on a hand-me-down bus. George Washington Carver had conducted his famous research on the peanut at this all-black institution some 50 miles away from Lewis's home. Lewis's visit there during grade school marked the first time he had traveled beyond the borders of Pike County, the place of his birth.

Lewis was born in 1940 on a sharecropper's farm outside of the county seat, Troy. When he was four, he moved with his family from this white landlord's property to a 110-acre farm of their own. At times his mother made the 50-mile trip to the state capital Montgomery and earned money doing household labor there. Otherwise she worked at home along with Lewis's father. John Lewis was the third of ten children, seven boys and three girls. His family lived in a three-room house that had no running water, no electricity, and no central heat. At any given point, Lewis shared a bed with two or three of his brothers. Behind their house was the barn, the smokehouse, and an outhouse. For toilet paper they used the pages of old catalogs (on good days) or dried up corncobs (when the catalogs ran out).

After he turned five, Lewis was put in charge of the family's flock of chickens. He cared for the birds, as anyone might do. But the young boy ministered to them, too, mimicking scenes from his church experiences with the Macedonia Baptist and Dunn's Chapel African Methodist Episcopal congregations. Lewis recited passages from the Bible to the chickens when they bedded down in their coop for the night. He delivered sermons to them while they rested on their roosts. When a chicken died, he gave it a funeral service, complete with flowers, a sermon of eulogy, and a sympathetic congregation of brothers, sisters, and cousins. Soon young John Robert Lewis had a nickname: Preacher.

Lewis was quite familiar with the Bible; it was the only book in his home. A large battery-powered radio served as the family's main link to the outside world during the days before television. Any food that wasn't raised on the family farm was purchased from the "rolling store man," a traveling salesman. Another regular visitor was the mailman. Both men were white. Lewis would be school-age before he visited nearby Troy with his father and saw any other white-skinned people.

The Lewis family raised cotton, peanuts, corn, and livestock on their farm. It was a labor-intensive group effort. John Lewis started working in the fields when he was six. By age 12 he was strong enough to help guide the mule-pulled plow. Everyone helped hoe and fertilize the crops and thin out extra seedlings. They picked cotton handful by handful, acre after acre, until all the plants were harvested. When farm chores conflicted with the school calendar, children were expected to stay home and work. Often Lewis did not. By his teenage years, Lewis was attending junior high and high schools located a school bus ride away from his home. Instead of farming, he would sneak off and catch the passing bus, leaving his share of the labor to other family members.

"I didn't like segregation," recalls John Lewis. "I didn't like racial discrimination. I detested it as far back as I can remember." Lewis encountered plenty of racism after he began to visit Troy, Alabama, near his family's farm when he turned six. For example, Negroes could attend movies at the local movie theater only if they sat in the balcony after climbing up the exterior fire escape (shown at left in above photo).

Several years earlier, in 1951, Lewis had taken what would become his only significant childhood trip. He traveled north by car with his Uncle Otis to visit relatives in Buffalo, New York. The pair brought along much of their own food and avoided restaurants, gas stations, and rest rooms that refused to serve Negro customers. In the North they saw Niagara Falls, toured cities where blacks and whites mingled freely, and stayed with relatives who lived in an integrated neighborhood of black and white residents. But such practices remained foreign back home in

Travelers in the South routinely encountered the separation of whites from Negroes (or colored people) during the mid-20th century. Those who rode buses and trains (before air travel was common) confronted "colored" and "white" seating sections as well as rest rooms (above in 1943), dining rooms, and motels. Often facilities for Negroes did not exist at all.

Segregation affected acts as trivial as buying a soft drink (right) or as significant as getting married. Water fountains, hospitals, ambulances, taxicabs, elevators, parks, swimming pools, jails, and cemeteries were either segregated (with whites receiving superior service) or else whites-only (with Negroes expected to do without).

the South. Even the landmark 1954 Supreme Court ruling on *Brown* v. *Board of Education*—which called for the end of separate schools for blacks and whites—brought no change to Lewis's world. The 14-year-old continued to ride the same hand-me-down school bus 20 miles each way to a segregated school where he was, by his own account, "an earnest student, but not an exceptional one."

There were a few glimmers of hope. One was the rising influence of Martin Luther King, Jr., whose preaching Lewis first heard on the radio in 1955. Another was the Montgomery bus boycott that began later that year as a nonviolent protest of segregation. By the spring of 1956, at age 16, Lewis was inspired to make his first protest against racism: requesting a library card at the all-white public library, and, when he was refused, recruiting signatures for a petition of complaint.

Although many people of his age were earning driver's licenses at this time, Lewis did not. He was so intimidated by the criticism of the white man who evaluated him during his behind-the-wheel driving test that he abandoned efforts to gain a license. Lewis may not yet have been driving, but by then he had preached his first sermon in a church (as opposed to in his chicken coop). He titled his sermon "A Praying Mother." Lewis spoke about Hannah's prayers in the Book of Samuel for a son whom she would raise with moral courage. News of his sermon made the Montgomery newspaper, his first ever news recognition. Lewis was days away from turning 16.

The next year Lewis applied to attend American Baptist Theological Seminary in Nashville, Tennessee, so he could train to become a minister. The school charged no tuition. Lewis won a spot among the small, all-Negro student body. Thus it was that in the fall of 1957, at the age of 17, John Robert "Preacher" Lewis began a journey. Standing five and a half feet tall, he climbed aboard a bus—not a handmade wooden one, but a silver-and-blue Greyhound bus—and headed north out of Alabama to the bordering state of Tennessee.

Following the segregation laws of the times, John Lewis took a seat at the back of the bus.

James William Zwerg (above left with his older brother in front of their house on Parkway Boulevard) was born on November 28, 1939, at St. Elizabeth's Hospital in Appleton, Wisconsin. At the time his hometown boasted some 28,400 residents. Exactly one person was listed in the 1940 census as being a Negro; nine were members of other races. Everyone else in the town was white.

"This little light of mine, I'm gonna let it shine.
This little light of mine, I'm gonna let it shine.
This little light of mine, I'm gonna let it shine,
Let it shine, let it shine, let it shine."

—freedom song

White America

JAMES WILLIAM ZWERG was born just three months earlier than John Lewis, but the contrast between their childhoods was so great that he might as well have been born into another world. Among the most noticeable differences was color—or the lack of color. "In the '40s and '50s, you need to understand that Appleton was 'lily white,'" says Jim Zwerg when he recalls his childhood in his Wisconsin hometown. "When it came to really getting *any* kind of an understanding of relationships with people of color, I didn't have it."

Zwerg was three or four years old before he saw his first African American, a black child whom the innocent Zwerg assumed was just a white-skinned person in need of a bath. That encounter occurred in Manhattan, Kansas, while Zwerg's father was training there for World War II military service. Zwerg attended kindergarten in Kansas (at a segregated school) then moved back home to Wisconsin. His Appleton school was all-white, too, but not because of segregation. There were no parallel facilities for blacks in his hometown because, like so many small towns beyond the South at that time, there were virtually no blacks living in the community. Throughout the rest of his childhood Zwerg rarely encountered racial diversity.

"I've tried to think back if my parents went out of their way to talk about other races as such, and I don't recall their doing that," says Zwerg. "What I remember was having ingrained in us: all men are created equal...that love was the most important commandment, that there is good and bad in all people." He adds: "I cannot think of anytime where my parents...said anything negative about another race, another religion. There was a lot of tolerance in our home in that regard."

Zwerg's father returned safely from World War II in 1945 and resumed his practice as a dentist. Jim Zwerg was five years old. He had one sibling, a brother three years older named Charles. His mother, a former schoolteacher, did occasional substitute teaching during Zwerg's childhood, but otherwise she served as housewife and mother in the typical pattern of so many middle-class families from that era. She read books aloud to her sons, managed the household chores, and served as den mother when her children entered the Boy Scouts.

"I had a wonderful childhood," recalls Zwerg. His family moved several times, but Zwerg mostly grew up in a comfortable, two-story white frame house on Parkway Boulevard. The brothers shared a bedroom (with twin beds) and had a rec room in a full-size basement, complete with a complicated layout for electric trains. In addition to electricity, the house had running water (with three bathrooms) and central heating. Out back was a detached garage that housed the family car and a sizable workshop.

Jim Zwerg (bottom left, top photo) and his family spent 16 months in Manhattan, Kansas, while his father—a dentist and oral surgeon—trained at Fort Riley for World War II duty. Dr. Zwerg went on to serve as a military dentist on the Fiji Islands of the Pacific. The rest of the family returned to their home in Appleton while he was overseas. The Zwerg family enjoyed listening to records and the radio, and writing or reciting poetry to one another.

During his childhood the local newspaper reported on a number of milestones small and large in the life of Jim Zwerg—from his election to student government posts to participation in the "clash of the classes" quiz bowl to his role as an acolyte, or altar boy, at his family church. Zwerg (third from right, bottom photo) held the post during his junior high days.

"My mother had ingrained in us that we...do nothing to cause any negativity towards my father's profession or his position. And as a result we were pretty straight-laced kids."

—Jim Zwerg, 2004

The Zwergs lived a short distance away from a community swimming pool in sizable Erb Park (top photo). A YMCA was nearby, too. The Zwerg boys played with other kids in the neighborhood, built treehouses, and flew kites in vacant lots. They enjoyed a series of new bikes, as well. Jim Zwerg even had his own car during high school. Chores for the boys included dish washing, lawn mowing, and snow shoveling.

Jim Zwerg (back row, center, wearing glasses, bottom photo) attended Philmont Scout Camp in 1956, between his sophomore and junior years of high school. By then he had already attained the coveted top rank of Eagle Scout. Scouting "met the requirements of being Dr. Zwerg's boy," he explains, recalling how he was encouraged to invest his energy into praiseworthy activities.

The Zwerg home was just blocks away from neighborhood elementary and junior high schools, multistory brick structures. Electricity, indoor plumbing, and central heating were a given there, too. Jim Zwerg did well with his studies. However, his skinny and tall frame (eventually he would pass the six-foot, one-inch mark) did not lend itself to sports. Wearing glasses for nearsightedness didn't help either.

Instead Zwerg won election to student leadership posts, worked on the yearbook staff, and acted in high school theater productions.

The Zwergs took a number of family vacations. They drove east to visit Washington, D.C., and they drove west to see Yosemite and other national parks. Dr. Zwerg once took his sons on a fishing trip to Canada. The family owned a summer cottage on Lake Winnebago near Appleton and shared a cabin in Wisconsin's north woods with other relatives. Zwerg grew up with easy access to swimming, boating, and fishing. Over the years his family owned a series of horses, too.

Boy Scouts played a major role in Zwerg's childhood. Zwerg progressed through the scouting ranks, attaining the top honor of Eagle Scout during ninth grade. He attended regional Scout camps (where he met a few Negro campers), became a Scout counselor, and traveled to New Mexico as a camper at the Philmont Scout Ranch (all of his fellow campers there were white).

The Zwerg family attended the First Congregational Church in Appleton, one of the city's larger congregations. Jim Zwerg sang in the choir and joined the church youth group. When, as a high school student, he attended a statewide camp for young Congregationalists, all the other participants were, per the norm, white. As he grew older, Zwerg became interested in a possible career in the ministry. He shadowed one of his church pastors during parishioner visits and soon, as a high school senior, preached his first sermon. Zwerg chose to speak about how "going to church is a little bit like getting your battery recharged."

During high school Zwerg worked part time at a local drugstore. Later on he worked for Appleton's streets department. Zwerg used some his earnings to purchase 100 acres of land. He and his family slowly planted trees as a timber crop on the property. He later used profits from selling this land to pay for his graduate school education.

There was never any question about whether or not the Zwerg sons would attend college. Both parents were graduates of local Lawrence University. Charles Zwerg enrolled at the University of Wisconsin in Madison. Jim Zwerg stayed in state, too, but he chose to attend Beloit College, a private liberal arts school about 150 miles southwest of Appleton. When Jim Zwerg arrived on campus in the fall of 1958, he found diversity at last—or at least a little bit of it. Out of a student body of nearly 1,100 students, there were, as Zwerg recalls, six students of color, five men and one woman.

Before long Zwerg was singing in a vocal quartet with three of the black men. They called themselves the "Sophisticats." Another black student, Bob Carter, was one of his freshman roommates. The two became friends, and Zwerg began to get an education in racism. Although many classmates accepted Negroes with the same openness as did Zwerg, some did not. Zwerg overheard racially based comments directed at Carter and watched as some white students moved to other tables if the pair tried to sit with them. When Zwerg realized that he had inadvertently pledged to join a segregated fraternity—one that his black friend could not even visit—Zwerg returned his pledge pin and joined an integrated house. It was his first protest against racism. He was 18 years old.

"How is it that you don't lash out at these people?" he asked his roommate. "Why don't you get mad?" wondered Zwerg, who had inherited his father's hot temper. In response Carter handed him a copy of *Stride Toward Freedom,* Martin Luther King, Jr.'s, account of the use of nonviolence during the Montgomery bus boycott. Zwerg read the book.

Eventually Zwerg chose sociology, the study of society, as his college major. When Beloit began participating in an exchange program with Fisk University—a predominantly black school in Nashville, Tennessee— Zwerg applied to attend and was accepted.

Appleton's downtown was just blocks away from the Zwergs' home on Parkway Boulevard. Residents flocked there for community events such as the annual Christmas parade (above). Lawrence University, the school where Jim Zwerg's parents had met, was nearby, too, as were papermaking factories and related industries.

Thus it was that in the beginning of 1961, at the age of 21, James William Zwerg boarded a train (he had yet to travel by commercial bus) and headed south out of Wisconsin. When he reached his destination, he told a cab driver that he needed a ride to Fisk. The white cabbie drove his passenger only as far as the school gates. With the innocence of a newcomer, Zwerg excused the man's behavior as rudeness, not racism.

Then, unloading his baggage himself, Jim Zwerg stepped alone through the entrance into another world.

The lunch counter sit-in movement in Nashville (above) and other Southern cities served as a training ground for students who became leaders in the growing civil rights movement, including Diane Nash, James Bevel, Marion Barry, Julian Bond—and John Lewis. At times during the sit-ins, gangs of white youths taunted the students, pulled their hair, poured hot drinks and other food on them, and snubbed out lit cigarettes on their skin. The students' nonviolent response to such abuses cast a negative light on segregation.

"Guide my feet while I run this race.

Oh guide my feet while I run this race.

Guide my feet while I run this race,

'Cause I don't want to run this race in vain."

—freedom song

Common Ground

EVERYTHING CAME TOGETHER in Nashville. It was not just the arrival
there in 1957 of John Lewis or in 1961 of Jim Zwerg. It was larger than
the story of two people. Perhaps it was the coincidence of a moment.
Maybe it was destiny or fate. Some credited the work of a divine hand.
Later on John Lewis would suggest that the "Spirit of History" had
intervened. Whatever one called it—and whether it was by design or
accident—just the right mix of people, events, circumstances, and beliefs
came together to make history at that time in Nashville.

It all started in February 1960 with nonviolent sit-ins at the segregated lunch counters of the South. In Nashville hundreds of students—
John Lewis included—took part in protests that would become the
most visible, well-organized, and sustained demonstrations in an effort
that spread to more than 100 cities. Spontaneity played a part in

many of the sit-ins, including the opening one in Greensboro, North Carolina, on February 1, 1960. Those in Nashville, however, grew out of events dating back to September 1958.

That fall John Lewis was immersed in his second year at American Baptist Theological Seminary. Even as he prepared himself to become a minister, though, Lewis observed a growing push—now labeled a movement—for the civil rights of the American Negro. "Wherever you went, it seemed, the talk was of the movement," recalls Lewis 40 years later in his memoir, *Walking with the Wind*. "'Free by '63'— you heard that slogan everywhere."

At that point John Lewis stepped into the movement with the help of James Lawson, a seasoned veteran of nonviolence. Lawson, a Negro, had gone to jail rather than fight in the Korean War, for example. He had lived in India, as well, and had studied the teachings of Mohandas Gandhi, the father of that nation's nonviolent revolution against Great Britain. Lawson, a newcomer to Nashville in the fall of 1958, began offering workshops on nonviolence to young people. Lewis attended them from the beginning. "This was stronger than school, stronger than church," recalls Lewis. "This was the word [of God] made *real*, made whole....I truly felt—and I still feel today— that [James Lawson] was God sent."

The workshops continued for more than a year and prepared surging numbers of Nashville students, black and white, to challenge the community's segregated lunch counters, which they did beginning on February 13, 1960. Their efforts persisted through months of rudeness, threats, violence, delays, arrests, and jailings. They gained the attention of the national television and print media. Reporter Chet Huntley concluded an hour-long NBC documentary by observing: "What we are witnessing today is a new kind of militancy and with it a new kind of soldier." In mid-April 1960, even before the NBC

John Lewis (above) earned his own room (for the first time in his life) and his meals at American Baptist Theological Seminary by scrubbing pots in the school cafeteria three times a day.

"It's a pleasure to have you down here, in fact we'd like you down about six feet," suggested one foe to stand-in participant Jim Zwerg (right), as a visiting student at Fisk University from the North.

report had aired, Lewis and the other nonviolent soldiers won a victory: the support of Nashville's white mayor. Key stores began admitting blacks to their lunch counters soon after.

The next school year, Lewis's final year at American Baptist, the students continued their workshops, planning, and segregation challenges. By this time the so-called Nashville Student Movement functioned like a well-oiled machine of disciplined and committed participants. A Central Committee, made up of veteran protesters

> *"This movement is not merely a demand for eating places...but a demand for respect....We will meet the capacity to inflict suffering with the capacity to endure suffering....We will wear [segregation] down by our capacity to suffer."*
>
> —Martin Luther King, Jr.
> April 20, 1960, speaking at
> Fisk University, Nashville, Tennessee

Nashville students applied the same principles of nonviolence in 1961 during stand-in demonstrations at local movie theaters (above) that they had used the previous year during lunch counter sit-ins. The students believed that love was the best antidote to violence and hate. Love "matches the capacity of evil to inflict suffering with an even more enduring capacity to absorb evil," they wrote in the statement of purpose for the Nashville Student Movement.

Nashville police officers arrested John Lewis for the first time on February 27, 1960. Other arrests and trials followed (at left, Lewis in court, second from right on March 28). A year later he celebrated his 21st birthday—behind bars. All across the South, students used this tactic of "jail, no bail" to call attention to their nonviolent protests against segregation.

like John Lewis, directed the close-knit but ever-expanding group.

Then, in January 1961, the student group gained one more member: Jim Zwerg. Something greater than logic or curiosity helped pull the Nashville newcomer into the movement. Zwerg credits the commitment of John Lewis, whom he met within days of his arrival in Nashville. "It was obvious that he had a very profound, deep faith," Zwerg would recall years later. He remembers thinking: "This kid is as young as I am, but boy has he got his act together."

By this point the Nashville students had a new target for nonviolent protest: the city's segregated movie theaters. Only one theater admitted Negro patrons at all, and then only through an alley entrance to its balcony. The students began holding stand-ins at the theaters. They waited in ticket lines, requested tickets, were refused (because they were black or because they were white and wanted to enter with black friends), then returned to the end of the line to repeat the process. Students might persist for hours, tying up ticket lines and highlighting discrimination in the process.

In a matter of weeks Zwerg progressed from being an observer to being a workshop participant (where he acted out both sides of the racial dramas) to standing in protest at movie theaters to remaining nonviolent in the face of attack. Later on he would be invited to join the Central Committee, becoming one of the few whites in this leadership group.

Violence—even when it left a student hospitalized—did not deter the students any more than it had during sit-ins the previous year. Racist white youths pelted the protesters with eggs, hard candy, rocks, snowballs, stink bombs, and bricks. They spit at them and threatened them. If the police stepped in at all, it was to arrest and jail the stand-in participants, not the hecklers and attackers. John Lewis went to jail (not for the first or last time). Jim Zwerg did not, but only because police never happened to arrest students where he picketed.

At stand-ins Zwerg earned special attention (meaning targeted abuse) as a "nigger lover"—the crude and disapproving label given by racists to a white person who sympathized with Negroes. Zwerg, who kept a journal of his experiences in Nashville, wrote in early February about his first time as a target of harassment. "I found that I had no urge to anger, but rather pity, for I realized that [my attackers] were not hurting me but themselves," he wrote. Two weeks later someone hit Zwerg in the head with a wrench or iron pipe. "Wham! Bang!" he recorded that night in his journal. "Ol' Zwerg is spinning, his glasses flying, and a swollen lip and bump on the head to boot." Other abuse followed, both verbal and physical.

The students may have been committed to their efforts, but few of their parents supported the idea. Parents feared for the safety of their children. They worried as well that the students might lose their hard-earned college spots. (Most campus officials backed the student efforts, though.) Some worried that the stigma of being arrested would tarnish their child's future. Others feared for their own safety if word filtered home of the actions of their sons or daughters.

Lewis's relations with his parents had been strained since the sit-ins of the previous year. "I lost my family that spring of 1960," noted Lewis in his memoir. His parents were "shocked and ashamed. My mother made no distinction between being jailed for drunkenness and being jailed for demonstrating for civil rights." Lewis recorded how his mother responded to the news of his first arrest with a letter that said: "You went to school to get an education. You should get out of this movement, just get out of that mess."

Zwerg's parents reacted with a similar tone. "I received a letter from my folks yesterday," Zwerg noted in his journal during March 1961. "They just don't understand....Yes I have obligations to my parents, but I have also obligations to my own children and grandchildren.

Freedom songs such as "We Shall Overcome" helped fuel the civil rights movement. When thousands gathered in Nashville at the climax of the sit-in protests, Guy Carawan (with guitar, left) played his new version of this old hymn. Student leaders familiar with his new lyrics sang along. David Halberstam, on hand as a young news reporter, later recalled how "verse followed verse….The students now had their anthem."

Who wants his or her children to grow up in a land of inequality?"

Both young men ignored their parents' concerns and kept protesting. They were rewarded with an end to the theater segregation in early May. Zwerg celebrated by going to his first Nashville movie. "Below is the ticket stub," he noted, taping it into his journal. Zwerg added: "It was the best show I've ever seen." He viewed another film a few days later, sitting side by side with a Negro friend. Only days remained before Zwerg faced his final exams, the end of his experience in Nashville, and his return to Wisconsin.

Lewis, whose graduation loomed, had decided against becoming a minister. (This was another sore point with his parents.) Instead he planned to support the civil rights movement or do community service overseas. For starters he'd earned a spot on a "Freedom Ride" to test the segregation of bus stations in the South. Lewis already had received a bus ticket to Washington, D.C., starting point for the ride.

If these two young men thought their directions were set, they were wrong. Fate, the Spirit of History, or that divine hand had other plans.

It was time for John Lewis and Jim Zwerg to make history.

Blacks and whites alike referred to the Southern practice of segregation as Jim Crow, a phrase that originated with a 19th-century black or black-faced minstrel character who danced on command. On May 14, 1961, when Freedom Riders challenged Jim Crow segregation of interstate buses, a racist mob set fire to their vehicle near Anniston, Alabama (below). After the riders escaped their burning bus, they were attacked by men armed with bats, iron pipes, bricks, and rocks.

"Stand up and rejoice, a great day is here.
We're fighting Jim Crow and the victr'y is near.
Hallelujah, I'm a-traveling, hallelujah, ain't it fine?
Hallelujah, I'm a-traveling down freedom's main line."

—*freedom song*

Early Rides

THE FREEDOM RIDES did not begin in 1961. They did not even begin in 1947 with the first organized test of interstate bus segregation. As far back as the 19th century African Americans had challenged segregated seating on public transportation. Stories survive of Sojourner Truth being struck by a train conductor for refusing to give up a choice seat (she sued and the man was fired) and of Frederick Douglass clinging to a whites-only bench as he was pulled from a train (he is reported to have held on until the seat tore loose from the floor).

In 1946 the U.S. Supreme Court outlawed segregated seating during interstate travel with its decision in *Irene Morgan* v. *Virginia*. The next year two groups that promoted racial harmony—the Fellowship of Reconciliation and the Congress of Racial Equality (called CORE)—tested compliance with the ruling by taking what they called a Journey of Reconciliation. Participants sought to reconcile, or resolve, opposing viewpoints on racial segregation. Sixteen men and women, eight white, eight Negro, spent two weeks that April traveling by bus between 15 cities in Virginia, Tennessee, Kentucky, and North Carolina.

"We found…that the bus companies are treating [the Supreme Court] decision as if it did not exist," reported James Peck, a white participant who received the only beating of the trip. Twelve arrests (of participants, not attackers) were made during the journey. Eight riders served jail time for breaking state segregation laws at odds with the Supreme Court ruling. More than one had to work on a chain gang.

No other tests followed. With enforcement of the Supreme Court decision left up to local authorities, compliance lagged, especially in the South. So, more than a decade later, on December 5, 1960, the Supreme Court issued another transportation-related ruling: *Boynton v. Virginia.* This decision extended the 1946 ruling to include the depot restaurants and rest rooms that served interstate passengers. The following March, James Farmer, a participant in the 1947 ride and the new director of CORE, called for a test of Southern compliance with the new ruling. "Our intention," according to Farmer, "was to provoke the southern authorities into arresting us and thereby prod the Justice Department into enforcing the law of the land." He dubbed the effort "Freedom Ride 1961."

James Peck, veteran of the 1947 ride, now in his 40s, answered Farmer's call. So did John Lewis, who had just turned 21. "This is the most important decision in my life," he wrote in his application essay, "to decide to give up all if necessary for the Freedom Ride, that Justice and Freedom might come to the Deep South." Lewis won a spot on the ride, serving as the informal representative of the Nashville Student Movement. Eleven others from around the country joined the multiracial group. They departed May 4, 1961, with plans for

> "When white men and black men are beaten up together, the day is coming when they will walk together."
>
> —*Reverend Fred Shuttlesworth*
> *May 14, 1961, Birmingham, Alabama*

Advocates of segregation surrounded a bus of Freedom Riders arriving at Anniston, Alabama, on May 14, 1961, and physically blocked its departure (above) long enough to slash the vehicle's tires. Then the attackers pursued the wounded bus until its wheels went flat a few miles west of town. Eventually they set fire to the vehicle and beat up its passengers.

Members of the Ku Klux Klan, the White Citizens' Council, and others who supported white supremacy and segregation attacked Freedom Riders who arrived in Birmingham, Alabama, on Sunday, May 14, 1961. Only one photo (left) survives to document the violence. Others were destroyed when attackers ripped film out of journalists' cameras. Police excused their tardy response to the violence by claiming that most officers were off duty celebrating Mother's Day.

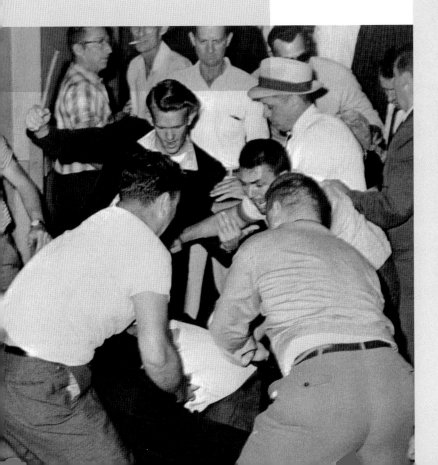

Freedom Riders who escaped the burning bus near Anniston awaited rescue (above) long after the fire was extinguished. Upon reaching the local hospital, all blacks were refused service. After a mob laid siege to the facility, Negroes from nearby Birmingham evacuated riders to safety.

a 13-day journey south to Georgia through Virginia and the Carolinas, then west to New Orleans via the Deep South states of Alabama and Mississippi. Riders agreed to serve jail time if they were arrested, and they expected to encounter violence. Some made out wills.

Five days into the ride, at Rock Hill, South Carolina, John Lewis received the first blow of Freedom Ride 1961. Young men hanging out at the local bus depot punched and kicked Lewis and a white companion after they entered the station's white waiting room. (Until then the main excitement of the trip had been the arrest of a Negro rider who refused to leave a shoe-shine stand in a whites-only barber shop.) Then, unexpectedly, Lewis was called away from the ride. Nursing a split lip and various other cuts and bruises, he flew to a spur-of-the-moment interview in Philadelphia for an overseas work experience.

On Saturday, May 13, the remaining riders gathered in Atlanta for dinner with Martin Luther King, Jr. The next day they planned to enter Alabama, the self-proclaimed "Heart of Dixie." This phrase was no mere license plate slogan. Alabama towns routinely posted welcome signs at their city limits emblazoned with the emblem of white supremacy groups like the Ku Klux Klan. Members of the Klan often served dual duty as police officers and civic leaders, collaborating to enforce the system of segregation.

The next day, which happened to be Mother's Day, Freedom Riders divided into two groups, one for each of the nation's leading bus companies: Greyhound and Trailways. The Greyhound group reached Alabama first, only to be attacked at Anniston by a racist mob that ultimately disabled their bus and set it on fire. When the Trailways passengers reached Anniston about an hour later, most segregationists were still engaged with their assault on the integrated Greyhound bus. However, eight hostile white men boarded the newly arrived vehicle and beat and dragged forward-sitting black passengers to the back of the bus. The attackers used fists, clubs, and Coke bottles to pound whites who objected. Walter Bergman, a 61-year-old white college professor who was participating in the ride with his wife, lay unconscious in the aisle as the bus sped toward its next stop—Birmingham, Alabama—with the racist hitchhikers still aboard.

In a prearranged deal, Birmingham police granted members of the

Klan and other segregationists 15 minutes to attack passengers when they arrived. With no law enforcement in sight, men assaulted James Peck, who had already been beaten en route. They "beat him and kicked him until his face was a bloody, red pulp," observed reporter Howard K. Smith, who happened to be in town preparing a story on segregation for CBS News of New York. The mob attacked Walter Bergman (only recently revived from his earlier beating), black passengers, innocent bystanders, and journalists. They broke the windows of a local radio reporter's car, interrupting his live broadcast and yanking him (and his microphone) out of the vehicle. Fifteen minutes into the violence, police officers appeared as if by magic, and the mob retreated.

Photos of the burning bus near Anniston made the national news and drew attention to the Freedom Rides from around the country (and the world). So did reports such as the one from CBS News. Many people viewed the attacks as an outrage against people who were, after all, only following national laws. However, quite a few others, especially many white Southerners, resented the challenge by the outside travelers and insisted that their state laws remained valid. A few of the attackers from Birmingham and Anniston were arrested for their parts in the violence, but none were convicted of any wrongdoing.

"We can't act as nursemaids to agitators," declared Alabama Governor John Patterson at a news conference three days later. "The state of Alabama can't guarantee safety of fools." The governor suggested the Freedom Riders sympathized with America's Cold War enemy, the Soviet Union, and favored communism over democracy.

"Every decent Southerner deplores violence," announced George Huddleston, Jr., a congressman from Alabama. "But these trespassers—these self-appointed merchants of racial hatred," he added, describing the Freedom Riders to his colleagues on the floor of the U.S. House of Representatives "—got just what they deserved."

More than two beatings and 50 stitches after entering Alabama, the decidedly unwelcome James Peck prepared to depart Birmingham (right). Although Alabama newspapers condemned the lawless mob that had attacked Freedom Riders ("Where Were the Police?" asked one front-page editorial), concern for the outsiders themselves was minimal. *"The issue is not protection of agitators but upholding the law of native white Alabamians against riot and violence,"* commented a Montgomery paper, using italics for emphasis. One reader wrote in "to personally thank the people who took part" in the recent violence.

"The going is getting rougher," James Peck admitted. "But I'll be on that bus tomorrow headed for Montgomery," he predicted, even as doctors used more than 50 stitches to close a four-inch-long gash across his forehead and five other cuts on his face.

In fact, however, he was not. Bus drivers refused to transport Freedom Riders out of the city, leaving them marooned at the depot within sight of hostile mobs. Ultimately the riders literally took flight out of Alabama, catching a plane to their final destination of New Orleans (and thus completing their trip ahead of schedule).

By all appearances, the Freedom Rides were finished.

"I couldn't believe how much blood there was," wrote John Lewis in his 1998 memoir, describing himself, Jim Zwerg, and William Barbee following their beatings in Montgomery. With blood still streaming from their wounds, Lewis revived Zwerg and Barbee then stood with them near the depot. Photographers, no longer threatened by the mob, snapped two pictures that appeared in newspapers around the world: a solo shot of the battered Zwerg (see newspaper pictured on page 51) and a companion image (above) of Lewis and Zwerg—black man beside white man—bloodied together as brothers in a common cause.

"If you miss me at the back of the bus, and you can't find
me nowhere,
Come on up to the front of the bus, I'll be ridin' up there.
I'll be ridin' up there, I'll be ridin' up there.
Come on up to the front of the bus, I'll be ridin' up there."

—freedom song

Blood Brothers

"WHEN THAT BUS was burned in Alabama, it was as though we had
been attacked," Diane Nash recalled years later. She and a number
of others from the Nashville Student Movement heard the news on
May 14, 1961, while celebrating the recent integration of local movie
theaters. John Lewis, en route from Philadelphia to Birmingham
(where he intended to rejoin the Freedom Ride), was among those
picnicking in Nashville when the story came in over a radio.

"Now comes the main thing," Zwerg wrote in his journal two days
later. "Some of us who are well-disciplined in nonviolence will
be taking a bus to Birmingham....You might say that it is a sympathy
ride." Ten student leaders—seven men and three women—from the
Nashville Central Committee planned to revive the Freedom Rides.
"You're going to get your people killed," warned John Seigenthaler,

administrative assistant to U.S. Attorney General Robert F. Kennedy. Coordinator Nash replied simply: "Then others will follow them."

John Lewis became group leader. Jim Zwerg, the only white male on the Central Committee, was one of two selected whites. "Those of us who will be going have a choice of expecting three things—jail, extreme violence, or death," Zwerg confided to his journal. At first Zwerg planned to travel without telling his parents, a strategy followed by Lewis. On the evening of their departure, however, as some students made phone calls, penned letters to family members, and wrote out their wills, Zwerg called home. The conversation did not go well.

"You can't do this," said his mother. "Don't go," she pleaded. Mrs. Zwerg reminded her son of his father's weak heart. (Dr. Zwerg had had his first heart attack while the youth was in high school.) "You've killed your father," she concluded. Then she hung up on her son.

Jim Zwerg did not waver. "I was never so certain of something in my life," he recalled years later. The riders departed Nashville early on Wednesday, May 17, bound for Birmingham, some 200 miles away. Just one week earlier Jim Zwerg had attended his first integrated movie. Now, fully expecting to be killed during his journey, he sat at the front of the bus beside Freedom Rider Paul Brooks, a Negro. At the Birmingham city limits, the pair was arrested for violating local segregation laws and hauled off to jail. Although the other students reached the bus terminal, within hours they had been arrested, too— so they could be placed in "protective custody," they were told.

The jailed students went on a hunger strike and sang freedom songs. The music bolstered their spirits—and irritated their guards. Plus it signaled others, now separated by race and gender (but still within earshot), of everyone's safety. Jim Zwerg found himself marooned in a cell full of local drunks. "Here's that nigger-lovin' Freedom Rider," his unsympathetic jailers had announced to the

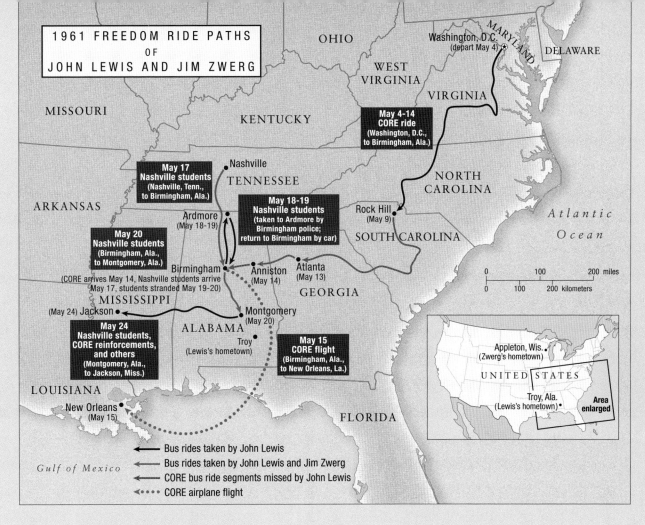

On May 4, 1961, an integrated group of Freedom Riders representing the Congress of Racial Equality (CORE) set out from Washington, D.C., to test Southern compliance with federal rules about interstate travel. After violence interrupted their trip on May 14, students from Nashville, Tennessee, initiated a Freedom Ride of their own.

whites, perhaps hoping the Southerners would rough him up. Instead Zwerg befriended the men to the point that they helped him try to signal the other riders. "Paul and Silas, bound in jail, got no money for to go their bail," the group sang. "Keep your eyes on the prize, hold on."

In the middle of the next night, some 24 hours after their arrests, Birmingham Police Chief Eugene "Bull" Connor personally escorted seven of the Freedom Riders in a convoy to the Alabama–Tennessee state line and instructed them not to return. The following morning, Friday, May 19, a Birmingham judge dismissed charges against Zwerg and Brooks, then warned them to leave town. (The tenth participant, another white exchange student in Nashville named Selyn McCollum, had been bailed out of jail by her father and escorted back to school.)

If Alabama authorities thought they had put a stop to the Freedom Rides, they were mistaken. Before the day was out, the seven outcasts had arranged for another Nashville student to pick them up and drive them back to Birmingham. They were reunited with Zwerg and Brooks at the bus depot. Reinforcements joined them—11 new recruits from Nashville and a student from Atlanta. Now there were 21 Freedom Riders waiting to travel through Alabama, including seven women (five black and two white). Zwerg remained the only white male.

An overnight standoff at the bus station followed. Bus drivers refused to carry the Freedom Riders. The students refused to leave the depot even as members of the Ku Klux Klan, wearing white robes but no hoods, roamed the depot. Local and state officials argued through the night with federal authorities and the bus company about what to do. Finally, on Saturday morning, May 20, after an 18-hour delay, students were permitted to board a Greyhound bus bound for Montgomery.

This time John Lewis and Jim Zwerg sat together at the front of the bus. The Freedom Riders departed at 8:30 a.m., accompanied by 32 patrol cars (16 in front, 16 behind), a surveillance airplane, various motorcycle-riding officers, and Floyd Mann, Alabama's public safety director. Mann had personally assured federal envoy John Seigenthaler that the riders would be safe from further mob attacks. Bringing up the rear were carloads full of news reporters. Violence, and the potential for further violence, had made the Freedom Rides national news.

All went well until the convoy reached the Montgomery city limits and found no local police escort awaiting it. The bus traveled downtown alone, then pulled into an oddly quiet Greyhound terminal not quite two hours after leaving Birmingham. Passengers began to disembark. Before John Lewis, as spokesman, could answer the first question of the assembled reporters, he was startled into silence. "People just

Only a handful of photos survived the May 20, 1961, mob violence in Montgomery, Alabama, including one of a Klan member (and off-duty police officer) attacking a news photographer (left). "The word was out: 'You will not take pictures of what's going to happen,'" Jim Zwerg later explained. "'There will be no press coverage.'"

Riots continued in Montgomery off and on for the next two days (below). When Freedom Riders, civil rights leaders, and local Negroes gathered for a mass meeting at the First Baptist Church on May 21, mobs surrounded the building and threatened its occupants for hours. At first federal marshals tried to hold back the mob. Finally the Alabama governor used National Guard troops to clear the streets.

"We have no intention of standing guard for a bunch of trouble-makers coming into our city making trouble."

—*L. B. Sullivan,*
Montgomery Police Commissioner
May 20, 1961, after failing to
protect arriving Freedom Riders

The view of Montgomery's Greyhound bus depot on May 25, 1961 (shown at left while under patrol by the National Guard), presented a stark contrast to the chaotic scene of five days before. During the May 20 riot, even as attacks ceased on the Freedom Riders themselves, members of the mob broke open their suitcases and used the contents to build a bonfire. People burned nearby parked cars and attacked innocent passersby, setting fire to the clothes of one black teen and jumping on his companion until the youth's leg broke.

started pouring out of the station, out of buildings, from all over the place," Lewis later recalled. Dozens, hundreds, soon more than 1,000 enraged people swarmed the area. John Seigenthaler, approaching the station by car soon after, observed "this almost anthill of activity" there.

Members of the mob carried baseball bats, metal pipes, lengths of rubber hose, pieces of chain, hammers, and sticks. Women armed themselves with heavy purses. Everyone shouted—"Git them niggers," "Get the nigger-lover," "Hit 'em, hit 'em again," and other commands —until the crowd seemed to take on one voice of roaring hatred. "It was like those people in the mob were possessed," Fred Leonard, a Freedom Ride reinforcement, later recalled.

Even in the madness, there was method. First the mob attacked the media, destroying camera equipment and knocking reporters to the ground. Next they turned on the Freedom Riders. Zwerg knew from experience that he, as the lone white man in the group, would likely draw the greatest wrath of the crowd: The only thing worse to these people than what they would call a "nigger" was a white sympathizer, a "nigger-lover," especially a male one.

Zwerg bowed his head and prayed. Then he experienced the greatest spiritual connection of his lifetime. "I immediately felt a presence with me. Not just that presence of my brothers and my sisters [on the Freedom Ride], but another presence. And a calm and a peace came over me that I knew if I lived or if I died, it was okay. It was gonna be all right." Then his beating began.

Mob members threw him over a railing, knocked him to the ground, kicked him in the back, and stepped on his face. Zwerg blacked out, oblivious to the continued assault. Attackers pulled him into a headlock and punched his face. Women pounded him with their handbags. When he slumped to the ground, people kicked him in the groin, ribs, and face, then hauled him up to repeat the cycle.

The assault on Zwerg added seconds to the attempted (and in a few cases successful) escapes of other Freedom Riders. The five black women riders departed in a segregated cab (but the Negro driver refused to carry the two white women riders). Some of the male students jumped over a fenced embankment and found shelter through the back entrance to the nearby post office. Others were thrown over the ten-foot drop, landed on cars parked below, and were beaten. Wave after wave of violence followed, and still no police arrived. A distraught Floyd Mann fought his way into the crowd.

When John Seigenthaler attempted to rescue the two stranded white females, men knocked him out with a blow from an iron pipe (fracturing his skull in the process). Lewis, trapped near Zwerg, recalls having "a conversation" with himself as attackers prepared to turn on him. "[I] said, this was it….I felt like I was going to die." Then whites knocked Lewis unconscious with a wooden crate. Nearby the mob attacked William Barbee, another new rider, stomping on him and kicking him. A reporter for *Newsweek* magazine observed a local Negro bricklayer stride into the melee and announce: "If you want to hit somebody, try me." So members of the crowd turned their fury on this new stranger (although attacks continued on Zwerg, Lewis, and Barbee, too).

Not until Floyd Mann reached Lewis and fired his handgun into the air did the mob pause in its fury. "There will be no killing here today," he stated. Intruders backed away from Lewis, but chaos continued to reign elsewhere. Next Mann forced the crowd back from Barbee, the bricklayer, and a besieged reporter. "One more swing and you're dead," Mann explained to one man wielding a baseball bat, cocking his gun beside the assailant's head. Finally, a hundred state troopers, responding to a distress call from Mann, began to arrive on the scene. So did local police, but only after having permitted ten minutes of rioting (in what turned out to be a prearranged deal with the Klan). Nevertheless sporadic violence continued for two more hours. Only when police used tear gas did the mob begin to disperse.

Medical care arrived even more slowly than had the police. Eventually a Negro cabbie hauled Lewis and Barbee to a hospital, but the driver dared not carry the white-skinned Zwerg. Whites-only ambulance drivers refused to appear, and whites-only hospitals declined to admit him. Zwerg remained at the scene for as long as two hours— sitting bloodied and senseless in the back of an abandoned, whites-only cab (its white driver having refused him service)—before he was finally removed from the scene. During the trip to the hospital, Zwerg revived enough to recognize the voices of white Southern men.

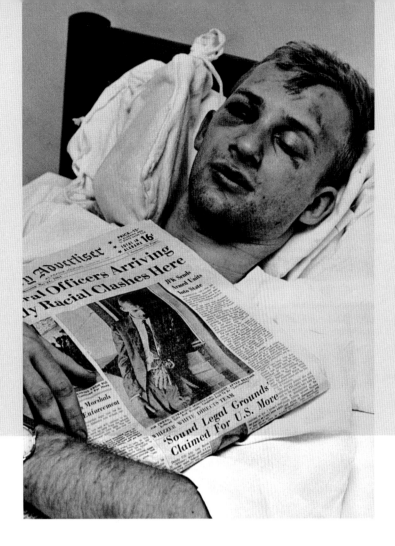

"I suppose a person has to be dead before anyone will call an ambulance in Montgomery," Zwerg (right) told reporters from his hospital bed there, still retaining a trace of his natural wit even as he groaned from the effort of talking. A nurse sedated him at one point during his hospitalization after hearing that a mob was approaching to lynch him. She wanted him to be unconscious in case the attack succeeded.

He assumed he was being taken to be lynched. In fact, Floyd Mann and two of his deputies were driving Jim Zwerg to a receptive hospital. Eventually 22 people received medical treatment following the Montgomery depot riot, including John Lewis, William Barbee, four news reporters, and federal envoy John Seigenthaler.

Perhaps Southern racists thought that the Freedom Riders—so beaten and scattered—had been defeated at last, but they were wrong again. That evening citizens, not just in Alabama but around the country, tuned into their nightly news and watched as Jim Zwerg, bruised and battered, lying flattened on his hospital bed, delivered a stunning statement:

"Segregation must be stopped. It must be broken down. We're going on to New Orleans no matter what. We're dedicated to this. We'll take hitting. We'll take beating.

"We're willing to accept death."

On Wednesday, May 24, the Freedom Rides resumed under heavy escort (above) en route from Montgomery, Alabama, to Jackson, Mississippi. Floyd Mann, the Alabama public safety director who had helped rescue riders four days earlier, supervised their security again as far as the border. Mann received a standing ovation during the May 21 mass meeting about the rides. A news commentator observed a mother waking up her child there "so he could stand up too and thank a white public servant who had done his duty."

"Ain't gonna let nobody, Lordy, turn me 'round,

turn me 'round, turn me 'round.

Ain't gonna let nobody, Lordy, turn me 'round.

I'm gonna keep on a-walkin', Lord, keep on a-talkin', Lord,

marching up to freedom land."

—*freedom song*

Rolling On

JIM ZWERG'S HOSPITAL bed statement, broadcast over national television, served as a clarion cry for action. It was as if the Pied Piper himself was rounding up volunteers. Individuals dropped what they were doing and headed off to join the Freedom Rides. Black and white, young and old, students, professors, members of the clergy, rabbis, Quakers, Northerners and Southerners, males and females alike, boarded trains, buses, and even airplanes bound for the segregated South—from Arkansas to Florida, from Georgia to Louisiana. Some came on their own; others were supported by a hastily organized Freedom Ride Coordinating Committee that recruited and funded participants.

State and federal authorities were furious. Neither side relished further violence or the continued collision of state versus federal authority. Alabama governor John Patterson challenged President

John F. Kennedy "to encourage these outside agitators to go home." Even Robert Kennedy, the U.S. attorney general, suggested that a period of cooling off seemed in order. But CORE's James Farmer replied that Negroes "had been cooling off for a hundred years. If we got any cooler we'd be in a deep freeze." The students agreed. "We couldn't stop," John Lewis recalls. "We couldn't turn back. We had to go, and we did."

On Wednesday, May 24, two buses departed Montgomery, four hours apart. They carried 27 Freedom Riders bound for Jackson, Mississippi, 258 miles away. (Jim Zwerg remained behind in the hospital.) Many of the new participants wrote out wills before their departures. Most riders stuffed notes into their clothes that would identify them if they were injured—or killed. State officials provided an overwhelming show of force for the trip, perhaps hoping additional riders would hesitate to follow such an apparently dangerous path. This time convoys stretched more than a mile in length while two helicopters and three airplanes flew overhead. National Guard soldiers rode aboard the buses, bayonets fixed to their rifles.

Hank Thomas, a veteran of the CORE trip through Anniston, rode with John Lewis on the second vehicle, a Greyhound. As the group neared Jackson, Thomas broke the rising tension by adding new words to a familiar song. "I'm taking a ride on the Greyhound bus line," he sang. "I'm riding the front seat to Jackson this time." Others joined in for the chorus: "Hallelujah, I'm a-traveling, hallelujah, ain't it fine? Hallelujah, I'm a-traveling down freedom's main line."

What the Freedom Riders did not know was that federal authorities had made a deal with state officials concerning their treatment. The states agreed to shield the riders from further mob violence (a relief to federal officials) and the federal authorities agreed to tolerate the arrest of riders (a tactic state leaders hoped would derail the rides

John Lewis (above, front), his head still bandaged from the beating he received three days earlier, led a press conference on May 23, 1961, with Martin Luther King, Jr. (right), and Ralph Abernathy (behind King), pastor of Montgomery's First Baptist Church. On May 21 Freedom Riders—disguised as choir members—were among those besieged during a mass meeting at Abernathy's church. "Bless all those cowards standin' outside," prayed a minister at one point during the rally. "Bless that stupid Governor of ours."

once and for all). Thus, when the two groups of passengers arrived in Jackson, authorities marched them through the terminal, into paddy wagons, and off to jail. They charged the riders with disturbing the peace for attempting to use white facilities, hoping that this indictment (as opposed to charges of violating local segregation laws) would hold up better against the recent Supreme Court ruling.

Once convicted, most of the Freedom Riders—including John Lewis—refused to pay any fines. Authorities sent them to jail. Over the next three weeks Mississippi officials shuffled Lewis and other riders from the Jackson city jail (which offered courtesy soap and towels) to the Hinds County jail (which allowed inmates to gather in a rec room)

Freedom Riders traveled under threats real (like jeering passersby, above) and imagined (including rumors of dynamite ambushes) during their May 24 trip from Montgomery to Jackson.

Armed escorts may have provided some sense of security for the first Freedom Rides to Mississippi (right). Even after state officials discontinued the guard details, however, new riders headed south. Media interest dwindled as the story turned away from headline-grabbing violence to tallies of jailings. Three-fourths of inmates were male; more than half were African American. Their attackers were never punished. Many citizens approved of the goals of the riders but did not necessarily approve of their methods; more than two-thirds of those surveyed condemned the rides.

"On a Greyhound bound for New Orleans
was such a gang you have never seen:
In rode the no-good 'freedom riders';
just a bunch of trouble-making outsiders."

—*sung by the Sunshine Valley Boys on*
WSFA-TV in Montgomery after
the city's May 20, 1961, riot

to the Hinds County prison farm (where there was a shortage of beds). Then, late one night, Lewis was among those transferred to the most dreaded destination in the Mississippi penal system: the state penitentiary and its Parchman Plantation.

At Parchman, armed guards patrolled on dawn-to-dusk work crews of slavery-style field labor. At various times they shocked Freedom Riders with cattle prods, sprayed them with water hoses to try to discourage their singing, removed their mattresses when they continued to sing freedom songs, tempted them with fried chicken and pecan pie to break hunger strikes, served them inedible food when they weren't on hunger strikes, and permitted them just one shower a week. Troublesome prisoners faced solitary confinement, time in sun-baked "sweat boxes," and restraint with wrist-breakers, devices that could be progressively tightened around someone's wrists. Inmates were issued no socks, no shoes, no pants—just an olive green pair of shorts and a T-shirt marked "Mississippi State Penitentiary." There were no blankets. Their only book was the Bible. They received no incoming mail and could only send out one letter a week. Lewis spent 27 days at Parchman and more than six weeks total in Mississippi jails.

Even as Lewis and his colleagues moved from one jail to the next, new Freedom Riders materialized to support the cause. Dozens, then hundreds, and finally more than one thousand people made Freedom Rides during the summer of 1961. Soon hundreds of them filled the jails in Mississippi and other Southern states. (Convicted Freedom Riders had their records cleared by the Supreme Court in 1965.)

Then, on September 22, 1961—after persistent prodding from the U.S. Department of Justice—the Interstate Commerce Commission (ICC) issued regulations that put teeth into the Supreme Court's *Boynton* v. *Virginia* decision of 1960. The ICC required depots to post notices that seating "is without regard to race, color, creed or national origin." Furthermore, any bus company that sent vehicles to segregated stations would be charged with breaking the law. New waves of Freedom Rides tested compliance with ICC orders after they took effect on November 1. Within three months CORE teams could report successful tests of 85 public transportation stations in the South. By the end of 1962, CORE declared the battle won against segregated travel.

At last, the Freedom Rides could stop.

Key participants of the Nashville-to-Birmingham Freedom Ride
gathered some months later to speak about nonviolence—and
to sing favorite freedom songs (above). Gathered are (from left)
Bill Harbour, Lucretia Collins, Jim Zwerg, Catherine Burks-
Brooks, John Lewis, and Paul Brooks.

"Only thing that we did right

Was to organize and fight.

Keep your eyes on the prize, hold on, hold on.

Keep your eyes on the prize, hold on."

—freedom song

Separate Paths

IN MAY 1961, Jim Zwerg's father saw the news reports of his son's condition and had a heart attack. Zwerg's mother suffered a nervous breakdown. (Both of them recovered.) Zwerg faded in and out of consciousness for 48 hours following his beating in Montgomery and remained hospitalized there for five days. He has no memory of the bedside news interviews that shocked his parents and helped launch a spontaneous mass movement.

On May 25, Jim Zwerg left the hospital to return to Wisconsin. His friends had departed for Mississippi the day before. Zwerg traveled home accompanied by his family minister; a security detail from the FBI escorted them as far as their airplane flight. The young man had plenty of healing to do. His injury tally included a severe concussion, a broken nose, at least one broken thumb (probably two), fractured teeth (more than half of them), countless cuts and bruises, internal trauma in his abdomen (never fully diagnosed), and three cracked vertebrae. There were less-visible wounds to heal, too, including damaged relations with his parents. These took longer to repair, although the trio managed to coexist. Many Freedom Riders, including John Lewis, faced similar family tensions over future months and years.

That summer—as Freedom Ride veterans healed, completed journeys, and emerged from jails—they made a shared discovery: they had become famous. Fan mail arrived at Zwerg's home by the box-full (along with occasional hate mail). Zwerg, Lewis, and others answered speaking requests. Various groups and institutions passed resolutions commending them. Then on September 27, 1961, the ten Nashville students who helped restart the Freedom Rides received a Freedom Award from Martin Luther King, Jr., and the Southern Christian Leadership Conference.

Following the ceremony in Nashville, King offered Jim Zwerg advice that set the course for his adult life. Zwerg, then a senior at Beloit College, had two conflicting career options in mind: a life in the ministry (as he'd earlier planned) or a leadership role in the civil rights movement (recently offered) helping with Negro voter registration. King tipped the balance with these words: "Jim, go in the ministry. You can touch an awful lot of lives, and the message needs to be spread in the Midwest, just as much as in the South."

Zwerg completed his college education and enrolled at Garrett Theological Seminary near Chicago. Professional counseling there helped him confront lingering effects from the Freedom Rides, including a slide into overconsumption of alcohol. He married Caroline Mueller in 1964. The next year he was ordained and took up a Wisconsin pastorate. Two sons and a daughter followed. In 1970, the Zwergs relocated to Tucson, Arizona. When, after ten years in the ministry,

"I love to sing. I love music," observes Jim Zwerg (left, during his years as a minister). In 1961 the choirboy-turned-Freedom Rider helped pass time before boarding the Greyhound bound for Montgomery by singing a solo from "Keep Your Eyes on the Prize." Zwerg notes that when the singing ended before a demonstration or rally, participants knew "we're together in this…here we go, by golly, we're gonna do this."

Zwerg was ready for a career change, he turned to community service and business. Eventually he held a management post with IBM, retiring in 1999. The Zwergs, their children, and their five grandchildren continue to live in Arizona. Zwerg's parents outlived the shock of their son's Freedom Ride by three decades (and came to accept it).

Zwerg's brief but intense involvement in the civil rights movement became a treasured memory. He shared his story with school groups and at club meetings. All the while Zwerg followed news of colleagues like John Lewis who remained on the front lines of the fight, occasionally wondering how his life might have changed had he gone to work in the South. As the years unfolded, a number of Zwerg's fractured teeth gave way (having a dentist father had helped save them for that long). He has lived with daily back pain since 1961.

RICHMOND HEIGHTS

> "You get knocked down, you get beaten, and you get patched up. And you come back for the fight.... You just continue to come back. You have to."
>
> —John Lewis
> May 12, 2004

On March 7, 1965, hundreds of demonstrators set out from Selma, Alabama, bound for the state capital to demand their right to vote. State troopers overran the group in a brutal attack that left leader John Lewis hospitalized (for the first and only time during his protests) with a fractured skull. Lewis (above, right) recovered in time to take part in a renewed (and successful) march later that month, accompanied by Martin Luther King, Jr., and his wife Coretta Scott King (together, center).

John Lewis lost his first bid for Congress in 1977 but went on to win in 1986 after staging a dramatic primary victory (left) over Julian Bond, another civil rights leader.

John Lewis combined involvement in the civil rights movement with further schooling. In 1967, he earned a degree in religion and philosophy from Fisk University in Nashville. By then he had participated in—and often led—key events in the struggle for African-American rights. Lewis chaired the Student Nonviolent Coordinating Committee (SNCC, pronounced "Snick") for three years, representing it as one of the "Big Six" planners for the 1963 March on Washington. His beating during the "Bloody Sunday" march across the Edmond Pettus Bridge of Selma, Alabama, helped hasten passage of the Voting Rights Act of 1965. By the end of his involvement with the civil rights movement, Lewis had logged at least 40 arrests.

In 1968 Lewis joined the presidential campaign staff of Robert Kennedy, the former U.S. attorney general. The year included horrific tragedy with the assassinations of Martin Luther King, Jr., and Robert Kennedy. It ended with great personal joy when John Lewis married Lillian Miles in a service conducted by King's father. Their only child (a son) was school-age before John Lewis righted one of the wrongs of his own childhood and earned a driver's license. He was 42. "Free at last, free at last," he told the officer who pronounced him road-ready. Another injustice was harder to shake: Lewis still avoids attending movies because "the memory of sitting up in that [segregated] balcony is just too strong."

In 1986 Lewis won election to the U.S. House of Representatives for Georgia's Fifth District. He has won every reelection bid since. Soon after taking office, Lewis crossed paths with someone else from the Freedom Rides: Gillespie "Sonny" Montgomery, commander of the National Guard troops that escorted Lewis's bus to Jackson, Mississippi. In the decades since this encounter, the lives of these two men, so divergent then, had evolved and aligned in an oddly fitting way.

Sonny Montgomery, like John Lewis, served the country as a member of the U.S. House of Representatives.

Toward One America

In 1989 John Lewis shook hands with Floyd Mann, the Alabama public safety director who had intervened during the Montgomery riot so many years before. The two had not met since. "Mr. Mann, it's good to see you again," Lewis recalls saying. Then he added, "Thank you for saving my life." The two men hugged and began to cry. "I'm right proud of your career," Mann told the congressman.

Both of these men—and the nation—had journeyed far since the Freedom Rides of 1961. Along the way the separate white and black worlds from the youths of John Lewis and Jim Zwerg had grown closer into one America. Jim Zwerg witnessed an example of the shift in 1986 while retracing the Freedom Rides for a 25th-anniversary documentary. On the approach to Montgomery, Zwerg happened to sit at the front of the bus beside a young African-American youth. The two began to chat. "Here was this young man who knew absolutely nothing about [the Freedom Rides]," recalls Zwerg. "It was very commonplace for him...to get on a bus that was being driven by a black bus driver and sit right up front....Did we accomplish something?" Zwerg asks himself. "Absolutely."

The Freedom Rides changed how people traveled. They revolutionized the civil rights movement by attracting young people and non-Southerners to the cause. They tested and strengthened future leaders of the struggle, both during the rides and with the jail time that followed. They even added a new phrase to the movement—Freedom Rider—a tag often given to people who put their lives on the line for the cause. But there were downsides, too. Competition developed between civil rights organizations. Violence grew from groups such as the Ku Klux Klan. In addition, some civil rights activists began to favor their own more militant action, too.

The bond of brotherhood remains strong between John Lewis and Jim Zwerg, even 40 years after their shared Freedom Ride (above). Says Zwerg of his friends from the era: "I love 'em like it was yesterday. All I have to do is listen to their voices, to hear a song, and it's right back there. And I hope it stays that way with me 'til the day I die."

"Forty years ago I participated in a movement that transformed my life forever. I never had a period in my life where my faith was as strong, my commitment as deep, my emotions higher. It was a period where I got to live on a special plane with some very special people."

—*Jim Zwerg*
September 18, 2002
from a lecture given at his alma mater,
Beloit College, in Beloit, Wisconsin

"We didn't give up. We didn't give in. We didn't despair. We kept the faith. We kept our eyes on the prize."

—*John Lewis*
February 8, 2005
from a lecture given at Lawrence University in
Appleton, Wisconsin, Jim Zwerg's hometown

John Lewis helped plan and speak at the 1963 March on Washington. Lewis (above, standing at center with other speakers) was just 23 years old when he asserted: "'One man, one vote' is the African cry. It is ours, too. It must be ours."

For Jim Zwerg, "the most intense, authentic moments of my life were in the movement....That was the mountaintop for me." Yet he finds himself nagged by personal doubts, even guilt, regarding the Freedom Rides. "How much of me is media hype?" he wonders. "I'm nothing special. I'm a dentist's kid from Wisconsin who happened to get on a bus with some friends who got the hell beat out of him. Think of the hundreds of kids...especially black students, that put it on the line and nobody knows their names." By being white-skinned, notes Zwerg, he drew extra attention among news reporters (who were themselves almost all white).

Many of the participants from the Freedom Rides gathered to commemorate its 40th anniversary in 2001, including John Lewis and Jim Zwerg. When the group visited the Birmingham Civil Rights Institute, Zwerg encountered a giant video monitor playing the clip of his hospital-bed broadcast from 1961. "I just started crying," he recalls. As Jim Davis, another ride veteran, comforted him, Zwerg stated: "I don't deserve this, really. I shouldn't be here....Everybody did so much more." Jim Davis disagreed, telling Zwerg: "Jim, you don't realize that your message from that hospital bed was the call to action for the country. Your words were the ones that inspired me to get on a bus."

Forty years earlier Jim Zwerg had drawn strength from another Freedom Rider: John Lewis. "If I had to pick one man that I wanted to stand at my side, I'd have to pick John," states Zwerg. "I knew he wouldn't break. John would be there; John would be the rock."

John Lewis, the rock, Freedom Rider turned congressman, spoke during the ride's 40th reunion about the importance of preserving and sharing memories from the civil rights movement. "We need to keep alive the sacrifices made by people who believed in positive change so long ago," he said. "The more we remind ourselves of what they did, the better off we'll be." John Lewis would be among the first to agree that further work is needed for the civil rights struggle to be complete. Yet, to those who might question whether enough progress has been made during his own years of memories, Lewis offers a challenge:

"Come and walk in my shoes," he says. "I will show you— America is a better place."

In 1963, just two years after the Freedom Rides, hundreds of thousands of Americans—black and white, young and old, representing all facets of the nation's profile—gathered as one to champion equality and human rights during the August 28 March on Washington.

PARTIAL ROSTER OF RIDERS

It is impossible to recognize the hundreds of volunteers from the Freedom Rides in a book so focused on two participants in particular. Yet so many people risked their lives and served time in jail to support the cause. The following roster presents a sampling of other Freedom Riders and their experiences. Accompanying photos were excerpted from the riders' Mississippi arrest records.

Nashville student **WILLIAM BARBEE** (who like John Lewis was enrolled at American Baptist Theological Seminary) was among those who volunteered to help restart the Freedom Rides. After the trip landed him in the same hospital as Jim Zwerg (one floor above in the Negro section), he echoed Zwerg's pledge to keep riding. "As soon as we're recovered from this, we'll start again," he promised. Yet, for Barbee himself, there would not be a full recovery. The blow he received to his head from an iron pipe on May 20, 1961, left him wounded permanently, emotionally if not physically. Some years later he would end his own life by, ironically, stepping in front of a bus.

MARION BARRY, eventual mayor of Washington, D.C., was among the swelling waves of volunteers who joined the Freedom Rides in 1961. Barry was well-known to early riders, having participated in the Nashville Student Movement while attending graduate school at Fisk University. In 1960 Barry became the first chairman of the Student Nonviolent Coordinating Committee (SNCC).

WALTER BERGMAN, the 61-year-old college professor who participated in the first CORE Freedom Ride, suffered permanent brain damage as a result of the beatings he experienced May 14, 1961, on the Trailways bus to Birmingham, Alabama, and at the depot. Soon afterward he suffered a stroke and became confined to a wheelchair for the rest of his life.

JAMES BEVEL, acting head in 1961 of the Central Committee of the Nashville Student Movement, handpicked the ten students who traveled to Birmingham and revived the Freedom Rides. On May 24 he joined them for the Montgomery-to-Jackson ride and a stay at the Mississippi penitentiary. He continued to play a central role in the civil rights movement following the rides. For a time he partnered in work and marriage with Nashville colleague **DIANE NASH**. Although Nash never actually traveled as a Freedom Rider, her behind-the-scenes organization made hundreds of trips possible for others. Nash moved to Jackson, Mississippi, for the summer of 1961 and monitored the arrival, arrest, and continued safety and whereabouts of hundreds of Freedom Riders.

PAUL BROOKS, Jim Zwerg's seatmate on the Nashville-to-Birmingham segment of the Freedom Rides, married fellow passenger Catherine Burks soon after. The pair took up work in the civil rights movement. Paul Brooks, like Jim Zwerg, turned to alcohol for comfort following the trauma of the Freedom Rides. Unlike Zwerg, Brooks drank until this abuse claimed his life.

When Police Chief Eugene "Bull" Connor removed Freedom Riders from his Birmingham jail and placed them in a convoy bound for the state line, **CATHERINE BURKS** ended up with John Lewis in Connor's car. She matched wits with the segregationist throughout the midnight trip, inviting him to join the students for breakfast. "You ought to get to know us better," she suggested. When Connor left his prisoners by the side of the road, Burks announced: "We'll be back in Birmingham by the end of the day." Bull Connor laughed, never expecting her words to come true.

STOKELY CARMICHAEL (later known by the name Kwame Ture) flew from New York to New Orleans in order to join the Freedom Rides on a Jackson-bound train. He turned 20 soon after while serving time at the Mississippi penitentiary in Parchman. Carmichael, a member of SNCC, took over its chairmanship from John Lewis in a 1966 shift by the group away from nonviolence. Later he promoted the concept of "black power."

WILLIAM SLOAN COFFIN, the outspoken chaplain of Yale University, reached Montgomery with other Northern clergy and college professors on May 24, 1961, the same day John Lewis and the first wave of riders headed on to Jackson. When Coffin's group integrated the depot with members of the local black clergy, all of them were arrested for disturbing the peace. They were the first Freedom Riders to inhabit Montgomery's jails.

LUCRETIA COLLINS was one of two black women chosen to restart the Freedom Rides from Nashville on May 17. One week later she was still with the ride, joining John Lewis on the second bus that traveled from Montgomery to Jackson. Collins conducted workshops on nonviolence among the new recruits on the trip, then walked off the bus with the rest of the riders and into paddy wagons bound for jail.

The death of his father took CORE leader **JAMES FARMER** away from the rides just as the buses left for Alabama on May 14. Farmer caught up with Freedom Riders in Montgomery. He sought to revive CORE's link to the rides there but did not plan to travel himself. However, at the depot 19-year-old student **DORIS CASTLE**, a CORE volunteer from New Orleans pleaded—"You're coming with us, aren't you, Jim?"—prompting Farmer to board the bus after all. He went on to serve time with John Lewis at various Mississippi jails, including at Parchman.

WILLIAM HARBOUR, born not far from Anniston in Piedmont, Alabama, was among the Nashville students who restarted the Freedom Rides on May 17. He was still riding a week later when the group approached Jackson, Mississippi. Harbour became Lewis's cellmate at Parchman soon after. In the decades that followed, Zwerg would correspond and visit more consistently with Harbour than any other of his friends from Nashville.

John Lewis, Jim Bevel, and **BERNARD LAFAYETTE** attended American Baptist Theological Seminary and worked together in the Nashville Student Movement. Lafayette continued to work for civil rights after the Freedom Rides, and he eventually introduced John Lewis to his future wife. Years later he returned to Nashville and served as president of his old seminary.

After Freedom Riders were attacked in Montgomery, **JAMES LAWSON** was among those who journeyed from Nashville to reinforce the effort. He joined the rides on May 24, serving as spokesperson on the first bus that headed from Montgomery to Jackson. Lawson, who had immersed Nashville students in the philosophy of nonviolence, objected to the heavily armed escort that accompanied his bus. "We would

rather risk violence and be able to travel like ordinary passengers," he insisted to a collection of reporters (who likely did not share his fearlessness).

FRED LEONARD was one of the second wave of Nashville students to join the Freedom Rides in Birmingham. He shared a cell at the Mississippi State Penitentiary with Stokely Carmichael. The pair resisted giving up their mattresses at Parchman (a punishment for their constant singing), with Leonard clinging to his even as guards hauled it from the cellblock. "I'm gonna tell God how you treat me," he sang as they pulled him along. The next fall as a student back in Nashville he collaborated with John Lewis on continued sit-ins and other protests against segregation.

Even though **SELYN McCOLLUM**, the white female on the Nashville-to-Birmingham trip, was pulled from the Freedom Rides by her father, she remained connected with the cause. On December 10, 1961, she and ten others tested compliance with the recently implemented Interstate Commerce Commission ruling. When they attempted to integrate the Albany, Georgia, train depot, they were arrested. Their imprisonment helped spark the "Albany Movement" for equal rights.

HANK THOMAS was a 19-year-old student at Howard University when he participated in the CORE ride. Even though he was arrested (for trying to eat at a white restaurant in South Carolina) and beaten (during the Anniston attack of the Greyhound bus) he helped continue the Freedom Rides with students from Nashville. "In 1961, I could not go into a McDonald's restaurant and buy an 18-cent hamburger," Thomas later recalled. Eventually he bought several of the restaurants.

Nashville minister **C. T. VIVIAN**, a supporter of the Nashville Student Movement, left home to join the rides in Montgomery without even consulting with his wife. He almost escaped arrest after arriving in Jackson on May 24. "I'm with them," he told the police captain, after emerging from the men's room to see his fellow passengers headed for jail. The imprisoned minister was beaten so severely by guards at a Mississippi county penal farm that embarrassed officials were forced to stop using the facility for Freedom Riders.

CHRONOLOGY

The following timeline notes key moments in the civil rights movement, the history of the Freedom Rides, and the lives of John Lewis and Jim Zwerg.

1939	1940	1946	1947	1955
James William Zwerg is born on November 28 in Appleton, Wisconsin.	John Robert Lewis is born on February 21 in Pike County, Alabama.	Supreme Court issues *Irene Morgan* v. *Virginia* decision, banning segregated seating on interstate buses and trains.	Journey of Reconciliation, sponsored by the Congress of Racial Equality (CORE) and Fellowship of Reconciliation, tests compliance with the *Morgan* v. *Virginia* ruling.	In December the Negro community of Montgomery, Alabama, organizes a yearlong boycott of segregated city buses.

1961

Jim Zwerg arrives in Nashville during January as an exchange student at Fisk University.

The Nashville Student Movement begins a stand-in campaign on February 1 to protest segregation in local movie theaters.

The CORE Freedom Ride departs Washington, D.C., on May 4 with John Lewis aboard.

John Lewis leaves the ride on May 9 to attend a job interview.

Violent mobs attack two Freedom Ride buses on May 14, destroying one of them in a fire outside Anniston, Alabama.

CORE aborts the Freedom Ride by flying participants out of Alabama on May 15.

Selected members of the Central Committee from the Nashville Student Movement, including John Lewis and Jim Zwerg, travel on May 17 to Birmingham, Alabama, with plans to revive the Freedom Rides; all are arrested and jailed.

Freedom Rides resume on May 20 with a trip from Birmingham to Montgomery, Alabama; Jim Zwerg and John Lewis are among those severely beaten when they arrive.

The governor of Alabama declares martial law on May 21 after mobs threaten to attack participants at a mass rally inside the First Baptist Church of Montgomery.

Freedom Rides resume on May 24 with a trip from Montgomery to Jackson, Mississippi; John Lewis is among those arrested when they arrive.

Jim Zwerg is discharged from a Montgomery hospital on May 25 and flies home to Wisconsin via Nashville.

John Lewis is among inmates transferred on June 15 from Jackson jails to the Mississippi State Penitentiary at Parchman.

John Lewis is among inmates released from Parchman on July 7.

Interstate Commerce Commission (ICC) rules on September 22 that communities must desegregate their transportation facilities by November 1 or be banned from use.

The Albany Movement begins in Albany, Georgia, in response to the December arrests of Freedom Riders testing compliance with the ICC ruling.

1968	1969	1970	1975	1976
John Robert Zwerg, the second son of Jim and Carrie Zwerg, is born on January 28. Martin Luther King, Jr., is assassinated on April 4 in Memphis, Tennessee. John Lewis marries Lillian Miles on December 21 in Atlanta.	Mary Patricia Zwerg, the only daughter and third child of Jim and Carrie Zwerg, is born on December 20.	The Zwerg family moves from Wisconsin to Tucson, Arizona, where Jim Zwerg takes up the pastorate for a new church. John Lewis becomes director of the Voter Education Project in Atlanta, Georgia.	Jim Zwerg resigns from the ministry and takes up work in the local business community.	John and Lillian Lewis adopt their only child, John-Miles Lewis.

1957

U.S. Congress passes the Civil Rights Act of 1957, the first legislation to support African-American rights since the 19th century.

● John Lewis enrolls at American Baptist Theological Seminary in Nashville, Tennessee.

1958

● Jim Zwerg enrolls at Beloit College in Beloit, Wisconsin.

James Lawson begins offering workshops on nonviolence to interested students in Nashville, Tennessee.

1959

Nashville students organize their efforts as the Nashville Student Movement.

1960

Four students in Greensboro, North Carolina, kick off the student sit-in movement with a protest at a Woolworth's store on February 1.

● Members of the Nashville Student Movement stage sit-ins at multiple local sites beginning on February 13.

Students from throughout the South gather in Raleigh, North Carolina, and organize the Student Nonviolent Coordinating Committee (SNCC), April 15-17.

Thousands of Nashville students and supporters march to City Hall on April 18 and demand an end to local segregation; the mayor speaks in favor of integration.

Supreme Court issues *Boynton* v. *Virginia* decision in December, banning segregated facilities at all terminals for interstate travel.

1963

John Lewis is among speakers at the March on Washington, held August 28 in the nation's capital.

1964

U.S. Congress passes the Civil Rights Act of 1964 to outlaw discrimination in voting, employment, and public facilities.

● Jim Zwerg marries Caroline "Carrie" Mueller on December 27 in Chicago, Illinois.

1965

● John Lewis (crouching on ground with hand raised) leads marchers across the Pettus Bridge in Selma, Alabama, and is severely beaten by state troopers on March 7, a day later known as "Bloody Sunday." Two weeks later Lewis is among those who complete the march to Montgomery.

● Jim Zwerg is ordained into the ministry on June 13. He takes up a pastorate in Wisconsin.

U.S. Congress passes the Voting Rights Act of 1965, assuring fairer access to the polls for millions of African Americans.

Supreme Court overturns 1961 convictions of Freedom Riders.

1966

James Gregory Zwerg, the first son of Jim and Carrie Zwerg, is born on March 2.

1977

● John Lewis runs for Congress and is defeated.

1986

John Lewis and Jim Zwerg are among those who commemorate the 25th anniversary of the Freedom Rides at a reunion in Nashville.

John Lewis runs for Congress and is elected to represent the 5th District of Georgia.

2001

John Lewis and Jim Zwerg are among those who commemorate the 40th anniversary of the Freedom Rides by retracing key stops along the route.

RICHMOND HEIGHTS

RESOURCE GUIDE

Books of General Interest

Boyd, Herb. *We Shall Overcome.* Naperville, Illinois: Sourcebooks, 2004. (Includes 2 CDs of historical audio clips.)

Bullard, Sara. *Free at Last: A History of the Civil Rights Movement and Those Who Died in the Struggle.* New York: Oxford University Press, 1993.

Carrier, Jim. *A Traveler's Guide to the Civil Rights Movement.* Orlando: Harcourt, 2004.

Carson, Clayborne (consultant). *Civil Rights Chronicle: The African-American Struggle for Freedom.* Lincolnwood, Illinois: Legacy Publishing, 2003.

Kasher, Steven. *The Civil Rights Movement: A Photographic History, 1954-1968.* New York: Abbeville Press, 2000.

Lewis, John. *Walking with the Wind.* San Diego: Harcourt Brace & Company, 1998.

Moody, Anne. *Coming of Age in Mississippi.* New York: Doubleday, 1968.

Books for Young Readers

King, Casey, and Linda Barrett Osborne. *Oh, Freedom! Kids Talk about the Civil Rights Movement with the People Who Made It Happen.* New York: Alfred A. Knopf, 1997.

McWhorter, Diane. *A Dream of Freedom: The Civil Rights Movement from 1954 to 1968.* New York: Scholastic, 2004.

Meltzer, Milton. *There Comes a Time: The Struggle for Civil Rights.* New York: Random House, 2001.

Miller, Jake. *Sit-Ins and Freedom Rides: The Power of Nonviolent Resistance.* New York: Rosen Publishing Group, 2004.

Turck, Mary C. *The Civil Rights Movement for Kids: A History with 21 Activities.* Chicago: Chicago Review Press, 2000.

Music and Videos, Including Companion Readers

Carson, Clayborne, et al. (editors). *The Eyes on the Prize Civil Rights Reader.* New York: Penguin Books, 1991.

I'm Gonna Let It Shine: A Gathering of Voices for Freedom. Round River Records, 1990.

Eyes on the Prize: America's Civil Rights Years, 1954-1965. VHS. Blackside Productions, PBS-TV, 1987.

Seeger, Pete, and Bob Reiser. *Everybody Says Freedom: A History of the Civil Rights Movement in Songs and Pictures.* New York: Norton, 1989.

Williams, Juan. *Eyes on the Prize: America's Civil Rights Years, 1954-1965.* New York: Penguin Books, 2002.

Places to Visit in Person and Online

African-American Odyssey
http://memory.loc.gov/ammem/aaohtml/

Birmingham Civil Rights Institute
Birmingham, Alabama
www.bcri.bham.al.us

Civil Rights Memorial
Southern Poverty Law Center
Montgomery, Alabama
www.splcenter.org/crm/memorial.jsp

Historic Places of the Civil Rights Movement
www.cr.nps.gov/nr/travel/civilrights/

Martin Luther King, Jr., National Historic Site
Atlanta, Georgia
www.nps.gov/malu

Montgomery Greyhound Bus Station Museum
Montgomery, Alabama
www.preserveala.org/greyhound.html

The Civil Rights Room
Nashville Public Library
Nashville, Tennessee
www.library.nashville.org/Newsevents/Civil%20Rights%20Room/civilrightsroom.htm

National Civil Rights Museum
Memphis, Tennessee
www.civilrightsmuseum.org

RESEARCH NOTES & ACKNOWLEDGMENTS

In May 2004 I spent two weeks retracing the route of the Freedom Rides that is chronicled in this book. My 4,000-mile journey took me from my home in Wisconsin to Washington, D.C., starting point for the Congress of Racial Equality (CORE) ride. From there I traveled south, stopping at key communities along the Freedom Ride route. I reached Montgomery, Alabama's, historic Greyhound Bus Depot on May 20, 43 years to the day after Freedom Riders were beaten there. (Although still boarded up when I saw it, the terminal is gaining new use now as a museum for the Freedom Rides.)

From Montgomery I detoured south from the route of the Freedom Rides to visit Pike County, birthplace of John Lewis. I stopped at Selma, Alabama, too, site of Lewis's 1965 beating. Then I picked up the trail of the Freedom Rides, passing through Jackson and Parchman, Mississippi, before turning into Tennessee to visit Memphis and Nashville. Throughout the trip I stopped at points of interest for the ride and visited historical sites, museums, and archives connected to the civil rights movement. Resources I collected along the way included ideas for photographs, copies of historical news clippings, and records from the office of Alabama Governor John Patterson, courtesy of the Alabama Department of Archives and History. I owe thanks to staff members at the Birmingham Civil Rights Institute, the Birmingham Public Library, the Troy (Alabama) Public Library, and the Nashville Public Library, as well.

A Traveler's Guide to the Civil Rights Movement by Jim Carrier helped keep me on course during my travels, and CDs of freedom songs provided the perfect soundtrack for the journey. I grew particularly fond of *I'm Gonna Let It Shine*, a production of Round River Records. My eyewitness tour of key places in civil rights history proved invaluable when I began to reconstruct the events of 1961. I am indebted to the Society of Children's Book Writers and Illustrators for helping to sponsor this trip by awarding me its 2003 Anna Cross Giblin Nonfiction Research Grant for a work-in-progress.

During my visit in Washington, D.C., I conducted photo research at the Library of Congress and interviewed John Lewis at his nearby office. Our conversation provided background to supplement his memoir from the civil rights movement, *Walking with the Wind*, a splendid resource in and of itself. I owe my thanks to Congressman Lewis and his staff for accommodating my interview and other requests. He and Jim Zwerg earn additional appreciation for reviewing this book in proof form and for writing forewords for it.

I traveled on three other occasions while researching this book, most notably a three-day trip in September 2004 to Tucson, Arizona, where Jim Zwerg and I literally talked for days. The lengthy transcript of our conversations became a key resource for this book. I am indebted to Jim (and his wife Carrie) for sharing time and memories so generously, both during that trip and in subsequent communications. Later on I made two trips to Appleton, Wisconsin, hometown of Jim Zwerg, so I could visit family landmarks, scour old newspaper files, search for possible photos, and attend John Lewis's speech at Lawrence University.

A number of books, in addition to *Walking with the Wind*, provided crucial background during my research. Taylor Branch presents a detailed account of the Freedom Rides in *Parting the Waters*. So, too, does *The Children*, a book written by David Halberstam, who as a young reporter for the Nashville *Tennessean* covered the sit-in movement in that city. Other principle sources among those listed in the accompanying bibliography include *Voices of Freedom*, an edited collection of oral history interviews; *The Struggle for Black Equality*, a scholarly assessment by Harvard Sitkoff; and the *Reporting Civil Rights* anthologies of period news accounts from the civil rights movement. Citations for all quoted material appear on page 76.

A project such as this one inevitably depends on the support and patience of family members who must cope with extended absences and tolerate the latest writing obsession of a parent or spouse. Thank you Dan, Sam, and Jake, for seeing me through another book. Others to acknowledge include Jim Zwerg's college roommate Bob Carter, Freedom Rider Bill Harbour, and Elizabeth Tardola—all of whom reviewed proofs of this book, the superb staff at National Geographic, members of my writing critique group, friends and relatives who hosted me during my travels, and others who forever encourage me to persevere. One last line of credit belongs to Harold R. Wilde, the man who started me on this journey in 1989 by suggesting I write a story for the Beloit College alumni magazine about Jim Zwerg, member of the class of 1962.

From small seeds do large plants grow.

CITATIONS

Abbreviations used below are FM (Floyd Mann), JF (James Farmer), JL (John Lewis), JP (John Patterson), JZ (Jim Zwerg), MLK (Martin Luther King, Jr.), and MZ (Mary Zwerg, mother of Jim Zwerg).

Forewords
p. 6, JL: "If not us, then who?" (Halberstam: p. 290)

*Chapter 1 / **BLACK AMERICA***
OPENING SONG: p. 11 (Harley: p. 3).

RAISED QUOTE: p. 12, JL: "The world I knew as a little boy…." (Lewis, 1998: p. 17).

PHOTO CAPTIONS: p. 12, JL: "Eight to ten hours of stooping…." (Lewis, 1998: p. 30); p. 15, JL: "I didn't like segregation…." (Bausum, May 2004: p. 15).

TEXT: p. 11, JL: "We were gonna make a bus…." (Bausum, May 2004: p. 15); pp. 11-13, JL: "It seems like buses…." (Bausum, May 2004: p. 14); p. 17, JL: "an earnest student…." (Lewis, 1998: p. 53).

*Chapter 2 / **WHITE AMERICA***
OPENING SONG: p. 19 (Seeger and Reiser: pp. 240-42).

RAISED QUOTE: p. 21, JZ: "My mother had ingrained in us…." (Bausum, September 2004: p. 40).

PHOTO CAPTION: p. 22, JZ: "met the requirements…." (Bausum, September 2004: p. 45).

TEXT: p. 19, JZ: "In the '40s and '50s…." (Zwerg, 2002: p. 1); p. 20, JZ: "I've tried to think back…." (Bausum, September 2004: p. 47); p. 20, JZ: "I cannot think of anytime where my parents…." (Bausum, September 2004: p. 81); p. 20, JZ: "I had a wonderful childhood." (Bausum, September 2004: p. 14); p. 23, JZ: "going to church is a little bit like…." (Bausum, September 2004: p. 39); p. 24, JZ: "How is it that you don't lash out…." (Zwerg, 2002: p. 1).

*Chapter 3 / **COMMON GROUND***
OPENING SONG: p. 27 (Seeger and Reiser: pp. xviii-xix).

RAISED QUOTE: p. 30, MLK: "This movement is not merely a demand for eating places…." ("King Urges Sit-In's Continue….").

PHOTO CAPTIONS: p. 29, stand-in foe: "It's a pleasure to have you down here…." (Zwerg, 1961: pp. 53-54); p. 30, Nashville Student Movement statement of purpose: "matches the capacity of evil…." *(Voice of the Movement)*; p. 33, David Halberstam: "Verse followed verse…." (Halberstam: p. 232).

TEXT: p. 27, JL: "Spirit of History." (Lewis, 1998: p. 64); p. 28, JL: "Wherever you went…." (Lewis, 1998: p. 72); p. 28, JL: "This was stronger than school…." (Lewis, 1998: p. 76); p. 28, Chet Huntley: "What we are witnessing today…." (Huntley); p. 31, JZ: "It was obvious that he had…." (Bausum, September 2004: p. 92); p. 32, JZ: "I found that I had no urge to anger…." (Zwerg, 1961: p. 13); p. 32, JZ: "Wham! Bang! Ol' Zwerg is spinning…." (Zwerg, 1961: p. 29); p. 32, JL: "I lost my family that spring…just get out of that mess." (Lewis, 1998: p. 115); p. 32, JZ: "I received a letter from my folks…." (Zwerg, 1961: pp. 45-48); p. 33, JZ: "Below is the ticket stub…." (Zwerg, 1961: p. 98).

*Chapter 4 / **EARLY RIDES***
OPENING SONG: p. 35 (Seeger and Reiser: pp. 62-63).

RAISED QUOTE: p. 37, Fred Shuttlesworth: "When white men and black men are beaten up together…." (Branch, 1988: p. 423).

PHOTO CAPTIONS: p. 41, headline: "Where Were the Police?" ("People Are Asking"); p. 41, editorial: *"The issue is not protection of agitators…."* ("The Governor of Alabama a Mob Leader?").

TEXT: p. 36, James Peck: "We found…that the bus companies…." (Peck: p. 92); p. 36, JF: "Our intention…." (Sitkoff: p. 98); p. 36, JL: "This is the most important decision in my life…." (Lewis, 1998: p. 129); p. 40, Howard K. Smith: "beat him and kicked him until his face…." (Smith: transcript p. 30); p. 40, JP: "We can't act as nursemaids to agitators…." (Ingram); p. 40, George Huddleston, Jr.: "Every decent Southerner deplores violence…." (Smith: transcript p. 31); p. 41, Peck: "The going is getting rougher…." (Branch, 1988: p. 424).

*Chapter 5 / **BLOOD BROTHERS***
OPENING SONG: p. 43 (Seeger and Reiser: pp. 72-73).

RAISED QUOTE: p. 47, L. B. Sullivan: "We have no intention of standing guard…." ("White Mob Tears Bloody Path").

PHOTO CAPTIONS: p. 42, JL: "I couldn't believe how much blood there was." (Lewis, 1998: p. 157); p. 47, JZ: "The word was out…." (Zwerg, 2002: p. 13); p. 51, JZ: "I suppose a person has to be dead…." (Duke: p. 586).

TEXT: p. 43, Diane Nash: "When that bus was burned in Alabama…." (Hampton, Fayer, and Flynn: p. 82); p. 43, JZ: "Now comes the main thing…." (Zwerg, 1961: p. 104); pp. 43-44, exchange between John Seigenthaler and Diane Nash. (Halberstam: p. 286); p. 44, JZ: "Those of us who will be going…." (Zwerg, 1961: p. 104); p. 44, MZ: "You can't do this…." (Recalled by JZ, Bausum, September 2004: p. 109); p. 44, MZ: "You've killed your father." (Zwerg, 2002: p. 16); p. 44, JZ: "I was never so certain…." (Bausum, September 2004: p. 99); p. 44, jailer: "Here's that nigger-lovin' Freedom Rider." (recalled by JZ, Zwerg, 2002: p. 10); p. 45, JZ: song lyrics (Zwerg, 2002: p. 11); pp. 46–48, JL: "People just started pouring out of the station…." (Sitkoff: p. 103); p. 48, John Seigenthaler: "this almost anthill of activity." (Hampton, Fayer, and Flynn: p. 89); p. 48, racist shouts. (Lewis, 1998: p. 155; Zwerg, 2002: p. 14; "White Mob Tears Bloody Path"); p. 48, Fred Leonard: "It was like those people…." (Hampton, Fayer, and Flynn: p. 87); p. 49, JZ: "I immediately felt a presence…." (Zwerg, 2002, p. 14); p. 50, JL: "a conversation," "[I] said, this was it…." (Bausum, May 2004: p. 8); p. 50, bricklayer: "If you want to hit somebody, try me." ("Days of Violence in the South": p. 21); p. 50, FM: "There will be no killing here today." (Recalled by JL, Bausum, May 2004: p. 9); p. 50, FM: "One more swing and you're dead." (Halberstam: p. 312); p. 51, JZ: "Segregation must be stopped…." (Birmingham Civil Rights Institute, video display).

*Chapter 6 / **ROLLING ON***
OPENING SONG: p. 53 (Seeger and Reiser: pp. 74-75).

RAISED QUOTE: p. 56, "On a Greyhound bound for…." (Alabama news release for May 22, 1961).

PHOTO CAPTIONS: p. 52, news commentator: "so he could stand up too and thank…." (Kempton: p. 583); p. 55, minister: "Bless all those cowards…." (Kempton: p. 582).

TEXT: p. 54, JP: "to encourage these outside…." (Alabama news release for May 20, 1961); p. 54, JF: "had been cooling off for a hundred years…." (Sitkoff: pp. 108-09); p. 54, JL: "We couldn't stop…." (Bausum, May 2004: p. 7); p. 54, song lyrics: "I'm taking a ride…. (Lewis, 1998: p. 166); p. 57, Interstate Commerce Commission ruling. (Sitkoff: p. 110).

*Chapter 7 / **SEPARATE PATHS***
OPENING SONG: p. 59 (Seeger and Reiser: pp. 110-11).

RAISED QUOTE: p. 62, JL: "You get knocked down…." (Bausum, May 2004: p. 9).

PHOTO CAPTIONS: p. 61, JZ: "I love to sing…." (Bausum, September 2004: p. 148); p. 61, JZ: "we're together in this…." (Bausum, September 2004: p. 147).

TEXT: p. 60, MLK: "Jim, go in the ministry…." (Recalled by JZ, Bausum, September 2004: p. 131); p. 63, JL: "Free at last, free at last." (Lewis, 1998: p. 50); p. 63, JL: "the memory of sitting…." (Lewis, 1998: p. 36).

*Afterword: **TOWARD ONE AMERICA***
RAISED QUOTES: p. 65, JZ: "Forty years ago I participated…." (Zwerg, 2002: p. 16); p. 65, JL: "We didn't give up…." (Lewis, 2005).

PHOTO CAPTIONS: p. 65, JZ: "I love 'em like it was yesterday…." (Bausum, September 2004: p. 138); p. 66, JL: "'One man, one vote' is the African cry…." (Lewis, 1998: p. 219).

TEXT: p. 64, JL: "Mr. Mann, it's good to see you again…." (Bausum, May 2004: p. 9); p. 64, FM: "I'm right proud of your career." (Halberstam: p. 651); p. 64, JZ: "Here was this young man…." (Haruf: p. 12); p. 66, JZ: "the most intense, authentic moments…." (Bausum, September 2004: p. 106); pp. 66-67, JZ: "How much of me is media hype?... (Bausum, September 2004: p. 169); p. 67, JZ: "I just started crying….I don't deserve this…." (Bausum, September 2004: p. 137); p. 67, Jim Davis: "Jim, you don't realize…." (Recalled by JZ, Bausum, September 2004: p. 137); p. 67, JZ: "If I had to pick one man…." (Bausum, September 2004: p. 165); p. 67, JL: "We need to keep alive the sacrifices…." (Benn); p. 67, JL: "Come and walk in my shoes…." (Lewis, 2005).

Roster of Riders
TEXT: p. 70, William Barbee: "As soon as we're recovered…." (Branch, 1988: p. 450); p. 70, Catherine Burks: "You ought to get to know us better." (Halberstam: p. 295); p. 70, Catherine Burks: "We'll be back…." (Halberstam: p. 295); p. 71, Doris Castle: "You're coming with us, aren't you, Jim?" (Branch, 1988: p. 473); p. 71, James Lawson: "We would rather risk violence…." (Branch, 1988: p. 472); p. 71, Fred Leonard: "I'm gonna tell God how you treat me." (Lewis, 1998: p. 171); p. 71, Hank Thomas: "In 1961, I could not go into a McDonald's…." ("Freedom Riders Retrace Their Route: Internet transcript); p. 71, C. T. Vivian: "I'm with them." (Halberstam: p. 339).

BIBLIOGRAPHY

Alabama. Office of the Governor [John Patterson]. News release for May 20, 1961. Alabama Department of Archives and History (Montgomery, Alabama). Alabama Governor Patterson—Administrative Files, 1961.

————. News release for May 21, 1961. Alabama Department of Archives and History (Montgomery, Alabama). Alabama Governor Patterson—Administrative Files, 1961.

————. News release for May 22, 1961. Alabama Department of Archives and History (Montgomery, Alabama). Alabama Governor Patterson—Administrative Files, 1961.

————. News release for May 24/25, 1961. Alabama Department of Archives and History (Montgomery, Alabama). Alabama Governor Patterson—Administrative Files, 1961.

————. News release for May 29, 1961. Alabama Department of Archives and History (Montgomery, Alabama). Alabama Governor Patterson—Administrative Files, 1961.

————. News release for June 3, 1961. Alabama Department of Archives and History (Montgomery, Alabama). Alabama Governor Patterson—Administrative Files, 1961.

Bausum, Ann. Interview with James Zwerg, September 22-24, 2004, Tucson, Arizona.

————. Interview with John Lewis, May 12, 2004, Washington, D.C.

Benn, Alvin. "Freedom Riders Return." *Montgomery Advertiser* (Montgomery, Alabama), May 5, 2001.

Branch, Taylor. *Parting the Waters: America in the King Years, 1954-1963.* New York: Simon and Schuster, 1988.

————. *Pillar of Fire: America in the King Years, 1963-1965.* New York: Simon & Schuster Inc., 1998.

Brewster, Robert G. "Proud of Patterson." *Birmingham News* (Birmingham, Alabama), May 25, 1961.

Carmichael, Stokely [Ture, Kwame]. *Ready for Revolution: The Life and Struggles of Stokely Carmichael.* New York: Scribner, 2003.

Carrier, Jim. *A Traveler's Guide to the Civil Rights Movement.* Orlando: Harcourt, 2004.

Davidson, Bruce. *Time of Change: Civil Rights Photographs, 1961-1965.* Los Angeles: St. Ann's Press, 2002.

"Days of Violence in the South." *Newsweek,* May 29, 1961.

Dowe, Dan. O. "Agitators Facing 'Full Jails' Threat." *Alabama Journal* (Montgomery, Alabama), May 17, 1961.

Duke, Bob. "Two Mob Victims Ready to Die for Integration." *Montgomery Advertiser* (Montgomery, Alabama), May 21, 1961. In *Reporting Civil Rights,* part 1: *American Journalism, 1941-1963,* 585-88. New York: Library of America, 2003.

Durham, Michael S. *Powerful Days: The Civil Rights Photography of Charles Moore.* Tuscaloosa: University of Alabama Press, 2002.

Fairclough, Adam. *Better Day Coming: Blacks and Equality, 1890-2000.* New York: Penguin Books, 2001.

"Freedom Riders Retrace Their Route." CBS News, May 12, 2001.

"The Governor of Alabama a Mob Leader?" *Montgomery Advertiser* (Montgomery, Alabama), May 19, 1961.

Halberstam, David. *The Children.* New York: Ballantine, 1998.

Hampton, Henry, Steve Fayer, and Sarah Flynn. *Voices of Freedom: An Oral History of the Civil Rights Movement from the 1950s through the 1980s.* New York: Bantam Books, 1990.

Harley, Bill, editor. *I'm Gonna Let It Shine: A Gathering of Voices for Freedom.* Companion booklet for CD produced by Round River Records, 1990.

Haruf, Whitney. Interview with James Zwerg, December 15, 1993 (via telephone).

Huntley, Chet. "Anatomy of a Sit-in." NBC "White Paper" special report, 1960.

Ingram, Bob. "Patterson Vows Arrest for Integration Testers." *Montgomery Advertiser* (Montgomery, Alabama), May 18, 1961.

Kasher, Steven. *The Civil Rights Movement: A Photographic History, 1954-1968.* New York: Abbeville Press, 2000.

Kempton, Murray. "Tear Gas and Hymns." *America Comes of Middle Age,* 1963. In *Reporting Civil Rights,* part 1: *American Journalism, 1941-1963,* 580-84. New York: Library of America, 2003.

"King Urges Sit-In's Continue; Bomb Scare Clears Fisk Gym." Nashville *Banner* (Nashville, Tennessee), April 21, 1960.

Lankford, Tom. "Jailed 'Riders' Wait for Bus." *Birmingham News* (Birmingham, Alabama), May 18, 1961.

————. "Montgomery Mob Wreaks Bloody Horror." *Birmingham News* (Birmingham, Alabama), May 21, 1961.

Leifeld, Ellen, and Andrew Oppmann. *Fox Cities Memories.* Appleton, Wisconsin: *Appleton Post-Crescent,* 2003.

Lewis, John. "Get in the Way." Lecture presented at Lawrence University, Appleton, Wisconsin, February 8, 2005.

————. *Walking with the Wind.* San Diego: Harcourt Brace & Company, 1998.

Loory, Stuart H. "Reporter Tails 'Freedom' Bus, Caught in Riot." *Herald-Tribune* (New York) May 21, 1961. In *Reporting Civil Rights,* part 1: *American Journalism, 1941-1963,* 573-79. New York: Library of America, 2003.

Marable, Manning, and Leith Mullings. *Freedom: A Photographic History of the African American Struggle.* New York: Phaidon Press, 2002.

McFadden, John T. *The Open Door: A History of First Congregational Church, 1850-2000.* Appleton, Wisconsin: First Congregational Church, 1999.

Nelson, Jack. "Two Veteran Rights Leaders Ousted by SNCC." *Los Angeles Times,* May 17, 1966. In *Reporting Civil Rights,* part 2: *American Journalism, 1963-1973,* 491-94. New York: Library of America, 2003.

Noble, Phil. *Beyond the Burning Bus: The Civil Rights Revolution in a Southern Town.* Montgomery, Alabama: NewSouth Books, 2003.

Peck, James. "Not So Deep Are the Roots." *The Crisis,* September 1947. In *Reporting Civil Rights,* part 1: *American Journalism, 1941-1963,* 92-97. New York: Library of America, 2003.

"People Are Asking: 'Where Were the Police?'" *Birmingham News* (Birmingham, Alabama), May 15, 1961.

Seeger, Pete, and Bob Reiser. *Everybody Says Freedom: A History of the Civil Rights Movement in Songs and Pictures.* New York: Norton, 1989.

Sitkoff, Harvard. *The Struggle for Black Equality, 1954-1980.* New York: Hill and Wang, 1981.

Smith, Howard K. "Who Speaks for Birmingham?" CBS News, May 18, 1961.

Suggs, Ernie. "Taking a Journey on Destiny's Bus." *Atlanta Journal-Constitution,* May 13, 2001.

Voice of the Movement (newsletter). Student Nonviolent Movement (Nashville, Tennessee), March 20, 1961.

"White Mob Tears Bloody Path of Violence through Capital." *Birmingham News* (Birmingham, Alabama), May 20, 1961.

Williams, Juan, and Quinton Dixie. *This Far by Faith: Stories from the African American Religious Experience.* New York: HarperCollins, 2003.

Zwerg, James. "One Man's Civil Rights Story." Lecture presented at Beloit College, Beloit, Wisconsin, September 18, 2002.

————. "The Stand-in" (unpublished journal), 1961.

INDEX

ILLUSTRATION CREDITS

Abbreviations used below are BCRI (Birmingham Civil Rights Institute), BN (copyright photos from 1961 by *The Birmingham News*, 2005, all rights reserved, reprinted with permission), JL (courtesy John Lewis), JZ (courtesy Jim Zwerg), LC (courtesy the Library of Congress Prints and Photographs Division), MDAH (Mississippi State Sovereignty Commission Records, Mississippi Department of Archives and History), NPL (Nashville Public Library, the Nashville Room), OCHS (Outagamie County Historical Society, Appleton, Wisconsin), and TPL (courtesy Troy Public Library, Troy, Alabama). Some images are reprinted again as spot art; additional locations are indicated in parentheses below.

Front cover, upper, LC-USZ62-125958 and Bettman/CORBIS; front cover, lower, LC-USZ62-118472 and Bettman/CORBIS; p. 1, BN; p. 2, LC-USF33-20522-M2; p. 9, Paul Schutzer/Getty Images; p. 10, JL; p. 12 upper, TPL; p. 12 lower, TPL (p. 11); p. 15, TPL; p. 16 upper, LC-USW3-037919-E; p. 16 lower, LC-USZ62-116815; p. 18, JZ; p. 21 upper, JZ; p. 21 lower, JZ; p. 22 upper, OCHS #P82-90-90-1 (p. 19); p. 22 lower, JZ; p. 25, OCHS #P82-84-80-79; p. 26, LC-USZ62-126236 (p. 73); p. 29 left, JL; p. 29 right, JZ; p. 30 upper, Henri Cartier-Bresson/Magnum Photos; p. 30 lower, Nashville *Tennessean*; p. 33, NPL (p. 27); p. 34, BN; p. 37 upper, BCRI Merrill Col. #9; p. 37 lower, Bettman/CORBIS; p. 38, BCRI Merrill Col. #32 (p. 72); p. 41, BN (p. 35); p. 42, LC-USZ62-117558; p. 47 upper, Donald Uhrbrock/Getty Images; p. 47 lower, Joseph Scherschel/Getty Images; p. 48, Bettman/CORBIS (p. 43); p. 51, Bettman/CORBIS; p. 52, Bruce Davidson/Magnum Photos; p. 55, Bruce Davidson/Magnum Photos; p. 56 upper, Bruce Davidson/Magnum Photos (p. 53); p. 56 lower, Paul Schutzer/Getty Images; p. 58, JZ; p. 61, JZ; p. 62 upper, Bettman/CORBIS; p. 62 lower, Bettman/CORBIS (p. 59); p. 65, courtesy of Greyhound Lines, Inc.; p. 66, Getty Images; p. 68, Bettman/CORBIS; pp. 70-71, MDAH SCR ID # 2-55-2-70-1-1-1 (Bevel), 2-55-3-71-1-1-1 (Burks), 2-55-2-83-1-1-1 (Collins), 2-55-2-68-1-1-1 (Lafayette), 2-55-3-68-1-1-1 (Leonard), 2-55-2-73-1-1-1 (Vivian); pp. 72-73, in chronological order, JZ (1939), NPL (1957), JZ (1958), LC-USZ62-126236 (1960), BCRI Merrill Col. #32 (1961a), MDAH SCR ID # 2-55-2-84-1-1-1 (1961b), JZ (1964), LCUSZ62-127732 (1965a), JZ (1965b), LC-U9-27173 (1970), JL (1976), JL (1977), courtesy of Greyhound Lines, Inc. (2001); p. 80, Danny Lyon/Magnum Photos; back cover, upper, LC-USZ62-119919 and Bettman/CORBIS; back cover, bottom, LC-USZ62-117558 and Bettman/CORBIS.

Following page: "Come let us build a new world together" became the caption for this photo which appeared on a popular poster printed by the Student Nonviolent Coordinating Committee (SNCC). The photo was taken during the summer of 1962 while John Lewis (kneeling at left) led SNCC protests against segregation in Cairo, Illinois.

Ann Bausum is the award-winning author of National Geographic's *With Courage and Cloth: Winning the Fight for a Woman's Right to Vote, Our Country's Presidents,* and *Dragon Bones and Dinosaur Eggs: A Photobiography of Explorer Roy Chapman Andrews.* She lives in Beloit, Wisconsin, with her husband and two sons. Visit her Web site: *www.AnnBausum.com.*

One of the world's largest non-profit scientific and educational organizations, the National Geographic Society was founded in 1888 "for the increase and diffusion of geographic knowledge." Fulfilling this mission, the Society educates and inspires millions every day through its magazines, books, television programs, videos, maps and atlases, research grants, the National Geographic Bee, teacher workshops, and innovative classroom materials. The Society is supported through membership dues, charitable gifts, and income from the sale of its educational products. This support is vital to National Geographic's mission to increase global understanding and promote conservation of our planet through exploration, research, and education.

For more information, please call 1-800-NGS LINE (647-5463) or write to the following address:

NATIONAL GEOGRAPHIC SOCIETY
1145 17th Street N.W.
Washington, D.C. 20036-4688
U.S.A.

Visit the Society's Web site:
www.nationalgeographic.com